BAMN

By Any Means Necessary

Brought To You By

WARRIOR, BROWN HORNET, CLYDE C. COGER

authorHOUSE®

AuthorHouse™
1663 Liberty Drive
Bloomington, IN 47403
www.authorhouse.com
Phone: 1-800-839-8640

Published by AuthorHouse 11/21/2014

ISBN: 978-1-4969-1527-6 (sc)
ISBN: 978-1-4969-1526-9 (e)

C O N T E N T S

Introduction vii
- Humble Beginnings of the GroupThink
  Project-Group (GT) vii
- The Meaning of the Symbolism: The
  Sankofa Bird xiv

Chapter 1: Racism... 1
- What is Racism?..1
- What Is The Origin Of Racism? 5
- How Does This System Maintain Itself? 8
- White Supremacy - The Burning House 14
- Identifying Racism 16
- What Is The Solution?.................................... 19

Chapter 2: From The Illuminati to the Hood 22
- What Is The Illuminati?..................................22
- Illuminati to the Hood..................................30

Chapter 3: The Disconnect 36
- Freek Philosophies...37
- Passive People..45

**Chapter 4: The Reconstruction of Black
                Civilization** **48**
- Health Consciousness.....................................48
- Unity...67
- Wealth Consciousness 74

Chapter 5: Contributing Authors Commentary... 79
- Warrior 80
- Brown H0rnet...88
- Clyde C. Coger, Jr... 102

Chapter 6: Destee Network.................................. 106
- Black People Web Sites... (Destee Network) 106
- Other Notable Links 106
- Suggested Reading and/or Viewing 107

Conclusion...111
- Front Cover Image of Malcolm X.................. 111
- Bibliography.. 113
- Poem: Mystery in History ...By Sister
  Phynxofkmt 117

INTRODUCTION

Humble Beginnings of the
GroupThink Project-Group (GT)

Various members of *Destee.com*, a discussion forum website on the Internet which is owned, operated and designed by and for Black People over the past fourteen (14) years; united on October 14, 2008, at 10:00AM with the idea of transforming the question of a discussion thread into material that would provide mental liberation for our people. Through *consensus based resolutions*. The members became the Origin of Racism Group, and later adopted the name, GroupThink Project-Group (GT) under the following goals and guidelines:

Group Objective: (GroupThink) The Group identifies that, "a state of ignorance," is the central cause of post modern racism. And to that end seeks to disclose and reverse the "state of ignorance" with truth and education.

Format/Discipline: Utilizing Voice Chat, plans and goals will be reached through group consensus, by note-taking and factual research, achieving the objective. Mic flow will be from bottom/up, following proper Chat Room protocols. GroupThink participants are not expected to hold private chats nor indulge in texting while in GroupThink.

Discipline: Robert Rules of Order (as a guide only)

Group Size: To be effective, a limit of five members, at any one live session, participating in GroupThink is permissible.

Process and Development: Factual material, researched and settled by group consensus, will be tracked to and edited in the Thread: *What is the Origin of Racism*, until the Objective is achieved.

After which foundation a prototype producing black unity was formed by group consensus, which consists of determining **Clarity of Purpose** and identifying those **Issues that Divide Us** as a people. This became the agreed upon standard by which we would conduct our work; resulting in the quorum by-law below and three successful projects (A Store Front, Newsletter and a published book, *BAMN*):

"As discussed in the 9th meeting, December 11, 2008, topics such as (Religion, Barack Obama, Meat Eaters vs. Vegetarians, Matriarchal vs. Patriarchal), etc... need not hit the table, because they are irreconcilable

and will only divide us at this time. As a group of people, we are nowhere near coming to a consensus on any of the above-related subjects. When we come together, topics such as these should be put on the back burner, as issues that divide us."

This concept of converting forum dialogue between black people into a published work is new and perhaps never attempted before now. Many times, discussion forums create solutions that often find a resting place in what is considered archival records. The global nature of discussions occurring on Destee.com bring to the table a unique perspective in that members log in from various countries covering the African Diaspora. The identity of those posting in the forums, can either be revealed or selected as avatars and screen names of choice. The screen names often used reflect the person's inner motivation. Here are the screen names of those that contributed to this project during the different stages of its early development; A007, Ang-EL, Jahari Kavi, Keita, Phynxofkmt and SeekingMaat.

The discussion thread responsible for the idea leading to this new approach contained the question: *What is the Origin of Racism*; and was deemed appropriate for answering, in order to begin our people's final insurrection from the belly of the beast, and the shackles of racism wrapped around our minds. We call the project our *homegrown publication*. The work is titled: **BAMN: By Any Means Necessary*, and lifts to light, unknown aspects of the racism question, through which understanding its origin, arrives from consensus based resolutions researched by the contributing authors, brown_hOrnet, WARRIOR and Clyde C. Coger, Jr.

As representatives of the total group effort, we hope the reader finds this work gratifying and uplifting with useful solutions, as the battle to free our minds from the grip of perceived racism white supremacy, continues.

Uniquely, in Chapter 5 of the book, the *Contributing Authors Commentary* section, allows free-style composition that rivals literary freedoms enjoyed by authors of typical prose. The three (3) contributing authors exercise personal mannerisms, designed to shock the reader into a process of self solution. This section allows departure from GT's group consensus prototype, by which readers may be able to recognize the consortium effect of the work.

BAMN: By Any Means Necessary, was titled from direct involvement and participation of the Destee. com Community, and stands as a tribute to our beloved ancestor, Malcolm X.

Consensus Based Resolutions:

This prototype doesn't come from a vacuum, but instead, from our African ancestors. According to an article titled *African Management Methods*, appearing in *Reference for*

Business Encyclopedia of Business, 2nd ed.: DO AFRICAN MANAGEMENT METHODS EXIST? Here is the following excerpt on "**The Timelessness Principle**" to make it plain:

African decision making is actually based on three interwoven management methods: timelessness, consultation, and **consensus**. *Unfortunately, these three principles clash with three of our own managerial expectations.*

We seek individual decision makers, especially within commercial settings. Americans admire the ability to make decisions individually, and thus seek that same capacity in those with whom we trade. We dismiss decisions made collectively as vague or too difficult to achieve, preferring the swiftness of either authoritarian decisiveness or majority rule. We also seek timeliness. Americans admire swift decisions, even in unstructured situations. In U.S. slang, we "wing it," "think on our feet," and "take off." Finally, we admire individual risk-takers. Instead of asking, "why" when faced with hard decisions, we often ask "why not," assuming that each misstep will be correctable.

In contrast, most Africans prefer decisions to emerge through timeless consultation, until participants can reach **consensus**. *To be sure, an African executive can make snap judgments as swiftly as Americans can. Nonetheless, he is likely to remain aware of obligations to his extended family or clan. By acting alone, he flaunts that clan's collective wisdom. By consulting, he honors it.*

*An American businessman once phoned an African friend, seeking the translation of a single word from his native language into English. He was put on hold, then heard ten minutes of happy, shouted conversation with others in the background. With everyone in agreement, the African triumphantly gave the caller the translation. When asked why he didn't just translate instantly, he loftily informed the American that he needed to consult his comrades "to guarantee the best phrasing." That thought would never have entered the American's mind. The time the Africans took to reach **consensus** was irrelevant; they enjoyed the process. This incident illustrates all three aspects of African decision making. Most Africans find it psychologically more satisfying to reach decisions by ignoring Western time frames, consulting one another, and attaining consensus.*

*Nonetheless, **African timelessness causes American anxiety**. We don't mind moving slowly as long as we know there is a deadline. Africa's collective decision-making bothers us too. We never know exactly when it will end, because they don't know either. We also don't know how the whole process works, or even what goes on. One way to learn is to break it into stages, then examine each in detail. The model suggested here is both idealized and simplified. Nonetheless, it reflects all three of the principles that drive the decision-making process: timelessness, consultation, and **consensus**. Consider the Zulu method of decision-making. They call it ndaba (consulting).*

Read more: African Management Methods - benefits http://www.referenceforbusiness.com/encyclopedia/A-Ar/African-Management-Methods.html#ixzz1995v5fxb

*Bandung Conference:

Most of our conscious brothers and sisters that have been around the black movement for any length of time, are very familiar with Brother Malcolm X's comments on the Bandung Conference in his memorial speech, *Message to the Grass Roots*. Bro. Malcolm made reference to this very important gathering of basically black people; specifically, this first large-scale African/Asian conference took place on April 18–24, 1955 in Bandung, Indonesia.

The important thing for us to realize about the conference of those twenty nine (29) countries is that there had to be some level of cooperation. And so, once again, we have the excellent example of <u>consensus based resolutions</u> of agreement to consider and suggested by our beloved, Malcolm X.

According to an article on the Conference in the Encyclopedia Britannica, *"Major debate centered on the question of whether Soviet policies in Eastern Europe and Central Asia should be censured along with Western colonialism; a **consensus** was reached in which "colonialism in all of its manifestations" was condemned, implicitly censuring the Soviet Union, as well as the West."*

If we are ever to have black unity in large numbers, then we must adopt and return to our heritage of reaching **consensus** rather than on going debate ending in disagreement or no plan of action.

GroupThink Project-Group assembly

The Meaning of the Symbolism: The Sankofa Bird

The color scheme of this particular style Sankofa bird was put together by sister <u>River</u> of <u>Destee.com</u>

There may be some that are without full understanding of the term Sankofa and the avatar symbol cited on the book's cover. The Akans are of West Africa and a present-day culture of Ghana, couched in symbols of Wisdom, and Knowledge of their Heritage.

Taken from a local aphorism: There is nothing wrong with learning from hindsight.

The word Sankofa is derived from the words SAN (return), KO (go), FA (look, seek and take). This symbolizes the Akan's quest for knowledge with the implication that the quest is based on critical examination, and intelligent and patient investigation.

The symbol is based on a mythical bird that flies forward with its head turned backward and the egg in its mouth symbolizes the future. This reflects the Akan belief that the past serves as a guide for planning the future, or the wisdom in learning from the past in building the future.

The Akan believe that there must be movement with times but as the forward march proceeds, the gems must be picked up and carried forward on the march.

W.E.B. DuBois Learning Center http://www.duboislc. net/SankofaMeaning.html

CHAPTER 1

RACISM

In this first chapter we will address racism. Our purpose is not to dwell on racism because we realize that focusing on something only brings about more of it. But we do realize that in order to solve a problem, it must be identified. So we will identify racism (how it got here, what it is, and how to identify it) and then move on.

What is Racism?

This may seem like a dumb question to some. After all, racism has been around for ages. Many scholars have dealt with it, yet there still is a controversy on what it is. Is it hatred towards another race? Is it prejudging other races? Is it discriminating against another based on their race? Does it matter? Well first...

Let us look at the definition of racism.

According to the Concise Oxford English Dictionary Racism is:

> *noun*
> 1. *The belief that each race or ethnic group possesses specific characteristics, abilities, or qualities that distinguish it as inferior or superior to another such group.*
> 2. *Discrimination against or antagonism towards other races or ethnic groups based on such a belief.*

Notice that this definition is NOT the belief that ones own race is superior to all others (as we are often told). It is only the belief that different races have different characteristics that can make them superior or inferior to others.

Notice also that hating someone because of their race has absolutely nothing to do with this definition.

According to the Oxford Companion of The English Language, the Origin of this word is French (1930's). It was first defined as, *"The theory, belief doctrine or prejudice which asserts that distinctive human characteristics and abilities, including language are determined by race (especially as established through such broad physiological categories as Australoid, Caucasoid, Mongoloid, Negroid)."*

The Oxford Companion goes on to say:

> Although often presented as scientific, especially in the wake of Darwinism, such a theory serves to buttress the assumption that one's own race is superior to all others. It may follow from this that one's own race therefore has, among other things, the right to control (and, when deemed necessary, enslave and even exterminate) people of races that are taken to be inferior or undesirable.

> A racist viewpoint figured in the arguments used to justify European imperial expansion and what Kipling called 'the white mans burden'; it was taken to the extreme by the Nazis during the Second World War (especially against Gypsies, Jews, and Slavs), and continues to underpin the concept of white supremacy among such groups as the Ku Klux Klan in the U.S.

Then, the Oxford Companion throws in another definition that is as follows:

> Hatred and intolerance of, and discrimination against people of another racial group or groups:

This second definition had to have later been added, because it has nothing to do with the origin of the word. Are we here to say that this second definition is wrong? Consider the following:

Right now globally, the White Race of people account for less than 10% of the total population, yet, control the vast majority of wealth and resources. Why? The obvious answer is Racism. So... does hating another race give you control of their resources? Does prejudging another race give you control of their resources? Does even discrimination against another race give you control of that race's resources? The obvious answer is no.

Now of course you can whip their behinds and take their resources, but if you are only 10 percent of the population you will obviously have to have a system set up to control the remaining 90 percent. If not, the 90 percent will revolt and take back what is rightfully theirs.

So while a person can define racism in a lot of different ways, the following explanation is an irrefutable fact. Racism is a system of control! So if you are trying to liberate yourself from racism, then you have to liberate yourself from that system.

Dr. Claude Anderson describes racism as, *"A competitive relationship between groups of people that are competing for the ownership of wealth, resources and power. A group phenomenon... A team sport."* We would also interject that this competition is also for the conscious mind of the masses. Dr. Anderson describes racism as a constant, well-nurtured and well-supported practice... and it really is.

Now, the current system of racism we are living in (which is the only system that has existed with regard to race) is based on the idea that the White race is superior to all other races.

In order for a very small population of people to maintain control of a large population and its wealth, it has to keep the large population in a false state of consciousness. It has to be perceived that it is "OK" for them to do so in order to keep the larger population from rebelling.

Slavery is an example of this. You can have one slave master and 50 slaves. Based on manpower, those 50 slaves could easily revolt and free themselves from the master. So the slaves had to be kept in a false state of consciousness (feeling that they were inferior and helpless) to maintain order. This is why Negroes had to be created. And part of this creation process was to "call" themselves masters.

Now we know that Racism is a system of control based on the idea of White people being supreme. So what can be done about it? Should we try to get out of the system or should we try to change the idea that it is based on? One way to answer that question is to go back to the origin of it.

What Is The Origin Of Racism?

Now, keep in mind that we aren't asking what the origin of slavery or "one race fighting against another" is or what the origin of "one group of people doing wrong to another group of people" is. We are asking what the origin of Racism (the System of Control based on a false idea) is. The idea obviously had to come first.

In present day, it is easy to see how a White person may feel that they are superior by nature. As a matter of fact, it is difficult to see how a White person would not feel that way (at least subconsciously). This is because right now the White race controls the vast majority of the worlds wealth and power, and subsequently the public and private school systems that teach the falsehood that Whites discovered civilization, America, technology etc.

But when did this begin? If you study history you will realize that at the time white people first came on the scene, Black people (everywhere you looked) were a highly civilized group of people while at the time white people were practicing savagery. At one point in time Ancient Egypt (Kemet - Land of the Blacks) was known by EVERYONE around as "The Land of the Gods"(as G.M. James explains in Stolen Legacy). This included the Romans, The Greeks, The Persians etc. They perceived Black people as "Gods".

So what in the world could have given white people the idea that they were superior (and therefore had the right to control, enslave and exterminate Black people)? Exactly... Absolutely nothing. So truth be told, if the origin of Racism is the idea that one's race is superior to all others, then it never would have begun.

Eventually, Black people were overrun by the barbarians. Most notably of those where Alexander the Great, who conquered Kemet and then proceeded to steal all of the current knowledge there and claim it for his own. And to make a long story short, this is what allowed for the current view of Greeks as the founders of modern civilization.

Now this "view" of Greeks being the founders of civilization and Africans contributing nothing to society was very important. Because it caused prejudice! Right now, we live in a system that produces prejudice. When you go to school, you basically learn (in short) that the White man is God and that "we" are dumb Negroes, whose origin is of slavery.

Now we know that White people conquered, enslaved, tortured and murdered Black people, but what was the real reason? Because we now know that it wasn't because they felt that they were superior to the people who they called Gods and had the right to do so. Here are 3 ideas on that:

1. Without the manipulation of "darker" skin races, whites are subject to genetic annihilation.
2. White people viewed themselves as inferior and hated the original people of the planet.
3. It was simply in their nature to do so.

Anyway you look at it, the important point is this. There is nothing that you can do to convince a racist not to be racist. While you may be able to sway a prejudice person (one who prejudges based on what he/she has been taught or has observed), you will never convince a racist person not to be racist because that person's racism is not based on what they don't know about you, it is based on what they know about you.

There's no need to "prove" to White people that we are the original people of the planet and we had highly advanced civilizations long before a Caucasian was thought about. The people who control the mainstream media already know this. But they don't want you to know they know it. Why? Because if we take the idea that they believe that they are superior, we will spend all of our time trying to prove ourselves to them rather than becoming self reliant. And unfortunately, we can't change that idea (within this system) because we don't control the system.

How Does This System Maintain Itself?

Even after forcing Black people into producing free slave labor, the progenitors of racism knew that they had to create a system that would maintain itself. They used three main tools to do so.

1) Economics
2) Religion
3) Biology

These tools are what granted the European enormous success from slavery, because the minds of the slaves were "trained to be sustained."

At critical points throughout slave history in America, each of these tools were implemented in stages. In America, they were implemented exactly in the order seen above. This is mostly due to significant changes in history, with the civil war having the strongest impact.

And right now, Racism lives quite comfortably. Why?

Not because economics was used to keep Blacks working constantly, for the White's benefit, instead of their own... since they didn't have the 40 acres and a mule that was promised to them.

Slavery in America began as an economic means to help Europe out of its filth-ridden dark ages. Europe understood the power of the African and did what it could to steal and keep that power.

Secondly, not because of a switch from economics to religion, this was essential to the slave masters, for they needed something to keep the Black people in line and in fear. It was just before the civil war was when this switch began to take place.

The Europeans used the Bible and a hurricane of White images, White morality, and White perspective, mostly to trick the slaves into believing that they were cursed because of their skin. A blatant falsehood among many falsehoods that Europe created and mandated insured certain protections for what they were doing to black people.

This tool alone played a crucial part in affording the Europeans to win the world-wide slave trade race by a very huge margin.

Now keep in mind, there were many other minor tools used that fall under the transitional switch from economics to religion to name a few.

1) Whippings
2) Castration
3) Starvation
4) Murder
5) Rape

All of these things were done in the name of their White deity, with the Bible at arms length to solidify their actions... while forcing those of us in the area to watch in horror.

Slaves were instructed as follows:

1) To accept your station in life
2) Be humble and obedient
3) Work hard. Don't steal or lie
4) Look only towards life after death

Now, what is piercing, devastating, and to be blunt, an ace in the hole for this transition's unlimited success to this day… is what is known now as the Stockholm Syndrome.

This is where the captives not only identify with their captors, but end up sympathizing with them as well.

This is where Racism's fuel to keep burning is stored.

Considering all this and the Europeans effort and dedication, to the art of keeping black people divided (Check National Security Memorandum 46), unification becomes more of a dream than reality. And division is an essential key to keep conquering a people that rise in numbers quickly.

Stockholm Syndrome must be dealt with in order for unification to breathe life.

Though Black people in America (those who have not sold out), despise racism, fascism, and a long list of other isms. Though they keep trying to unify with other black people who have adopted other religions or other avenues of worship, the European and his powerful ally, Racism, has supplied Black people, with many luxurious illusions of freedom. This allows for a sense of security that is nothing more than a falsehood. How can one even think of unification if one is already sold on the slave master's version of freedom for Black people?

Third, not because of the switch from religion to biology, but since the impact of Charles Darwin's 1859 book, "On the Origin of Species," White people in America proudly accepted Darwin's evolutionary theories, which were said to prove that Black people were the lowest form of human, considering that Whites, who owned and controlled just about every aspect of America and Black people had nothing at all. Other than the shame of saying that they built America.

Racism lives comfortably, due mostly to the major differences between two types of Black people in America... the house Negro... and the field Negro. Malcolm X spoke on the difference.

The field Negro would notice Massa's burning house and his/her heart would rejoice because that field Negro needed the emotion of payback to the utmost level and would enjoy watching the oppressor suffer... even if it meant he/she too would suffer.

However, the house Negro didn't want Massa's house to burn because he loved every aspect of the Massa. The house Negro had a much deeper connection to Massa's

Family
Land
Overseers
Friends and relatives
Property

Values and his
Evil ways

This connection was blinding to the house Negro, allowing the house Negro to proudly look down on the field Negro (seeing himself as better, wiser or smarter)… and not pity him, but indeed see him as someone of ignorance, stupidity, and of lower form (often judging, plotting and tricking him for Massa).

Some of the same mentalities that existed during the time of physical slavery have filtered down from one generation to the next and still exist today. Keep in mind that slavery never ended, it just changed. It is now more of a mental state than it is a physical one. And the same structure still exists.

You've got your slave masters, your overseers, your house Negroes and your field Negroes.

1. Slave Masters (the few men at the top of the structure) who rule over all of the institutions (corporations, religions, school systems, political institutions etc.) and create, infiltrate and control the secret societies. They decide most of the major events of the world.
2. Secret Societies (Skull & Bones, Cap & Gown, Bilderberg Group, Council on Foreign Relations etc.) and government counter intelligence agencies.

3. House Negroes, which are the Black secret societies that are subservient to and advise the White ones (Boule etc. and the entities they control). They are there to keep the field Negroes in line by any means necessary. Some of the tactics used are spying, sniffing out the Black "messiahs", keeping Black people in a mental state of helplessness (always asking the overseers and masters to let them be equal, and save them from situations that the masters put them in, as opposed to becoming self reliant and controlling their own destiny) and keeping them engaged in and distracted by the current racist system. These house Negroes (similar to the days of open slave trading) are awarded many benefits.

4. Field Negroes. These are the masses of people who serve as the "batteries" for the white supremacist machine.

And to this day, those two ideologies (House Negro vs. Field Negro) are still at war to this very day over the same basic issue.

And that issue is...

White Supremacy - The Burning House

House Negroes want to keep it, dress it up and make it more beautiful. Field Negroes want to burn it down.

Dr. Martin Luther King Jr. was quoted as saying, "I fear I am integrating my people into a burning house." He said this during the turbulent 1960's. He was correct.

This current racist White supremacist system, this current state of false reality based on misinformation and the suppression of information has had a strong hold on planet earth for quite some time now. But we are entering a new age (an information age). And as more and more people wake up to what is really going on around us, the house burns faster and faster. But it's not going down without a fight.

America... the proud, the beautiful, and the free. These are the claims that a lot of White people and numerous other nationalities boast that America truly is. And to no surprise, a considerable amount of Black people with slave ancestry, will wager their lives on these claims... with full knowledge of Black people's condition... past and present. The consciousness of Black people in America has been so severely damaged that many of us see nothing wrong in how we are treated, or perceived.

Harriet Tubman was quoted as saying, *"If I could have convinced more slaves that they truly were slaves, I could have freed thousands more."* You can't break out of a system that you don't realize that you are in. Today's current system of slavery exists mostly in the mind. And those who do "wake up" and see the manipulations, the betrayals, the super-slick politics very clearly, and stand against it are singled out and targeted by the American government for trying to wake up the masses to what is going on around them. They have to be stopped in order to save Massa's house. And normally, it is the House Negroes who assist in the elimination of threats to the house.

There is a very long history of this, with the plight of Nat Turner definitely being a major example.

This burning house began on the blood of the indigenous people in America, and grew once more Black people were brought here through chattel slavery, and became dominant once the Civil War ended.

It's been burning strong ever since. Now add the accelerants of manipulation, betrayal, trickery, divisions, and politics... and you have a raging house fire that only a few can see. But, it can't burn forever before it falls. And those who are dependant on it will burn right along with it. But how can you see it?

Identifying Racism

Now, if you believe that we are not still living in a system of racism, then consider the following information. Systematic racism is a very difficult thing to detect. And because it is systematic, it is not something that happens deliberately in a lot of cases (outside of the people who maintain the system). For example, if someone where to start an "Adolf Hitler" holiday in honor of Hitler's achievements, that person would be considered "racist." However, Christopher Columbus (who makes Hitler look like a humanitarian) has a holiday that is celebrated in his honor every year and not too many people seem to have a problem with it.

Now, do most people celebrate Columbus because they hate Africans and Native Americans? No. Most people who celebrate Columbus Day do so simply because it is a holiday. And the masses celebrate whatever is given to them. This is why a lot of Black people celebrate and recognize July 4th as independence day (even though this is really the day that some White people got free from some other White people and would go on to decide that Blacks are 3/5 of human beings).

You see... that's just "The Way It Is" You see the White so called supremacists who run America don't believe that Blacks are really a part of or deserve to be a part of America. And therefore, Independence Day for America only applies to them. Whatever day Black people got free (if they ever really did) is up to them to celebrate separately. You see, whatever is White is "American" and whatever is Black is "Black" or "Black in America."

But, why are people not blowing the whistle on this? Well it is very simple. It is because the belief is that "White people are superior and therefore have the right to manipulate control and murder the less desirable races."

Even though the majority of people reject this notion on a conscious level, it is accepted on a subconscious level or otherwise these holidays wouldn't be accepted.

This type of ideology affects us everywhere. When you watch TV, if a show is predominately Black it is called a Black Show, but if it is predominately white, it is a show. If a movie is predominately Black it is a Black Movie. If it is predominately white, it is a movie. When the Ebony Experiment (John and Maggie Anderson's public pledge to try to exclusively support Black businesses) came out, many people said that it was racist. How dare somebody exclude other races and only do for themselves. But if you examine many of those who stated this, you would realize that most and close to all of the places that they shop, do business etc. are European owned. But it is not considered White nationalism. Why? Because, there is no such thing as a White owned business. It's just a business. They are just shopping where they are.

Quite simply we are dealing with the normalization of European dominance and systematic Stockholm Syndrome amongst black people. And anything that threatens the pecking order throws up a red flag. Not even because people hate Black people, but simply because that is "How It Is." There are a lot of Black folks who are afraid to do for themselves because they are "afraid" to be racist. They want to make sure to include everyone even though they are rarely ever included (outside of exploitation) with others.

If Black people ask for reparations, they are told to pull themselves up by the bootstraps, but if they decide to do so (via self support) they are told that they are racist. Any radical move that may change the pecking order is seen as out of order.

What Is The Solution?

Should we spend our time trying to be equal with White people, or should we spend our time trying to empower ourselves? Well, let's consider the first part of the question. Will Black people ever convince White supremacist to walk hand in hand with them?

Well... Let us take a look at genetics. If a Black (brown) personal mates with a White person, the baby will come out brown. This is because the genes of the brown person are dominant to the recessive genes of a White person. Surely you've known of and have seen some people who you would have thought were Black and never would have known they were mixed if they hadn't told you. But on the other hand, how many people do you know that look 100% European that you found out had a Black mother or father? As a matter of fact, when we are speaking in genetic terms, Black people are at the top of the food chain with the most dominant genes. Therefore, if there ever was a level playing field and the different races were put into a true "melting pot." What would happen to the White Race?

Dr. Frances Welsing states this in the ISIS Papers

> *"The genocide of non-Whites must be understood as a necessary tactic of a people (white) that is a minority of the worlds population and that, because it lacks the genetic capacity to produce significant amounts of melanin, is genetically recessive in terms of skin coloration, to the black, brown, red and yellow world majority. Thus, the global white minority must act genocidally against people of color for the purpose of white genetic survival. This is the "Kill or be Killed" Mentality."*

You see, the phrase "Once you go Black, you never go back" is not just an expression. It's the truth! And "They" know this.

Therefore, if you have this idea (which has been given to us) in your head that we are going to convince or educate White Supremacy to let us be equal and voluntarily commit suicide once they figure out that we aren't inferior, then you are naive to say the least. But that is the trick. If you believe that racism is the belief that one race is superior to another, and that the reason that White Supremacist are suppressing you is because they think they are superior to you (which is the excuse given), then your natural instinct will be to try to educate them and convince them that you are not inferior so they will stop oppressing you.

And that is just what most of us do. We constantly try to be equal with White people. Rather than moving toward self reliance, we move towards dependence. Our ideology is always "White people have this, but we only have this. So we need to keep bothering them until they give us this, and help us get this, then we can be equal with them (because they are the standard)." And of course the real question is, "What are we going to do if they say no?! Keep being a pest?" This is why we are always in the position of weakness and they are always in a position of strength.

So first, we need to change our perspective. If we spent half the time doing for ourselves as we do trying to "measure up" to White people we would be a lot better off. Freeing yourself from being discriminated against, being prejudged or being stereotyped is nothing but a PR move. And while Public Relations may land you a good job, it won't free you from the beast.

It is time to empower ourselves and move toward liberation and do so By Any Means Necessary for OUR people regardless of what "prejudice" or "racist" people think or tell us they think about us.

CHAPTER 2

FROM THE ILLUMINATI TO THE HOOD

Black People in modern times have always known that there was a mysterious force that seemed to be ruling over them. We have long used phrases like, "The Mann" "Mista Charlie," "The Establishment," "The Power Structure," "The Beast," etc. to describe White supremacy. And when referencing a Black person who is doing something detrimental to us, you may often hear the phrase, "That's what they want us to do." Or maybe, "That's all apart of the master plan." But whose master plan are we talking about. And who is the "they" that we speak of? Without that answer, we are lost. Because, "Them White Folks" aint gonna cut it!

What Is The Illuminati?

Now, we left off in chapter one speaking on the origin of this current system of systematic racism being when the

Greeks (under Alexander the Great) conquered Egypt. Now there had been many attacks on Kemet up to that point, but the Greeks took it further than anyone before them when they actually moved their capital from their homeland to Egypt. But something else very interesting happened during this timeframe. Armed with all of the knowledge that the Greeks had stolen, a man by the name of Demosthenes (a Greek statesman, a spy, and an orator of ancient Athens) started a Greek Patriot Society (a fraternal order). This was a secret society of Greek bloodlines that considered themselves to be "enlightened."

Demosthenes lived from 384-322BC. And the year of his death is honored to this day. These Greek bloodlines (tyrants) would continue to wreak havoc on the globe from that point forward (stealing, plundering and expanding their realm of power) for millennia to come.

These bloodlines go down through Alexander the Great, Julius Caesar, Ptolemy XIV, Herod the Great, and on down through the Roman Piso Family. These bloodlines also include Constantine the Great, King Ferdinand of Spain, Queen Isabella of Castile and on down through King James. It stretches through King George (1st – 3rd), King Edward (1st-3rd), Queen Victoria, King Edward the 12th, Queen Elizabeth (1st and 2nd) on down through Prince Charles and Princess Diana and Prince William.

This same bloodline also encompasses George Washington, John Adams, John Quincy Adams, Thomas

Jefferson, Franklin Delano Roosevelt, George W. Bush, John Kerry, Al Gore, et al.

But of all these, there are four main bloodlines (top dogs) that control 4 separate regions of the earth. These bloodlines are the Rhodes, Rockefeller, Rothschild and Oppenheimer families. These are the four families who are at most responsible for developing the global White supremacists power structure that we see today. Do the research on these families, and it won't be pretty.

But now, let's get back to the plot. These diabolical ones figured that in order to sustain and enhance their domination, they should consolidate. So, in the late 18th century a decision was made to organize these bloodlines into a formal group.

On May 1st 1776, sponsored by Mayer Amschel Rothschild, Adam Weishaupt (a professor at William and Mary College and a Jesuit), organized these so called elite bloodlines into a group in Bavaria Germany.

This group would be called, "The Order of The Illuminati." The term Illuminati had been used for centuries (by those bloodlines who considered themselves to be enlightened), but this was the first time that these groups were gathered into a central organization. The objective was then (and still is now) to form a New World Order (one world government) in which these bloodlines would monopolize the earth.

The official bloodlines were as follows:

1. Astor
2. Bundy
3. Collins
4. DuPont
5. Freeman
6. Kennedy
7. Li (Chinese)
8. Onassis
9. Rockefeller
10. Rothschild
11. Russell
12. van Duyn
13. Merovingian (European Royal Families)

Other families connected with this group are Rhodes, Oppenheimer, Disney, Krupp, Reynolds and McDonald.

This wicked enterprise would consist of Born Men, and Made Men. The Born men are those who are the direct descendants of the so called royal or enlightened bloodlines. And the Made men are those who fought and proved themselves to be gladiators (like Christopher Columbus).

This was an important transition. This transitioned the world from a period of time where it was simple caste system (Whites and the top, and Blacks at the bottom) to a system where the elite White Bloodlines now rule over the masses as a whole. White skin is no longer a ticket to prosperity. And while the caste system of so called White supremacy still exists, White people who step out of line get killed just like Black people. Now, it's all about the agenda.

A lot of White people are upset because their freedoms are being taken away by an elite secret group. But often what they don't realize is that the same people who they are fighting against are the same people who put them in a position of wealth, prosperity and superiority to begin with (including the so called forefathers). This is a matter of chickens coming home to roost.

This New World Order is the Symbol that you see on the back of the dollar bill. The Latin words "ANNUIT COEPTIS" mean "He (God) has favored our undertakings" The words below the pyramid explain the nature of this undertaking. The words are "NOVUS ORDO SECLORUM" which mean, a "New Social Order" or a "New World Order."

In short, these men feel that they can rule based on the false premises that they:

1. Are royalty, and have a covenant with God because they are the descendants of Pharaoh Akhenaton, and
2. They are the "chosen" ones because they are the direct descendants of the Tribe of Judah.

These men also feel that because they are enlightened, they are above law. They believe that the concept of right and wrong is to be applied to the masses (the inferiors who can't think for themselves).

But what is interesting is that the very knowledge that they possess that makes them feel superior is the very same knowledge that was stolen from the people they claim to be superior to.

This is why, just as Greek philosophy is stolen and perverted Egyptian philosophy, all of the Illuminati symbols (All Seeing Eye, Baphomet, The Swastika etc) are all stolen and perverted Egyptian symbols.

Adam Weishaupt the founder of Illuminati stated, "The strength of our Order (the Illuminati) lies in its concealment; let it never appear in any place in its own name, but always concealed by another name, and another occupation."

On December 5, 1776 Weishaupt opened up the first branch of the Illuminati using his own students. This chapter was Phi Beta Kappa (which is the parent of all fraternal systems in American universities today). Phi Beta Kappa existed as a secret society for years until there was pressure put on them from the Anti-Masonic party (founded in 1828). Phi Beta Kappa went public and is now an honors society.

Shortly after, the Illuminati re-emerged in America as Skull & Bones (The Brotherhood of Death) in 1832 at

Yale University. The co-founders of this society were William Russell (Connecticut State Legislator) and Alphonso Taft (U.S. Attorney General). Skull & Bones secret number is 322 (which is in honor of Demosthenes who died in 322BC).

The Skull and Bones philosophy is the "double-cross system." Hence the Crossbones symbol with the Skull. Anyone who is not in the loop (so to speak) can be double crossed (tricked, lied to, manipulated, etc) to further the insiders' agenda.

Some notable members of Skull & Bones are as follows:

William Taft (27th President of the U.S.), Russell Davenport (editor of Fortune Magazine), Pierre Jay (first chairman of the Federal Reserve Bank of New York),

Harold Stanley (founder of Morgan Stanley, investment banker), Britton Hadden and Henry Luce (co-founders of Time Life Enterprises), William Henry Draper III (Chair of United Nations Development Programmer and Export-Import Bank of the United States), Prescott Bush (U.S. Senator, father of George H.W. Bush and financier of Adolf Hitler), George H.W. Bush (41st President of the U.S. and the 11th director of the C.I.A.), George W. Bush (43rd President of the U.S.) and his cousin John Kerry (who ran against Bush and gave the American people a "choice" of who to vote for).

Adam Weishaupt was also quoted as saying, "By this plan, we shall direct all mankind in this manner. And, by the simplest means, we shall set all in motion and in flames. The occupations must be so allotted and contrived that we may, in secret, influence all political transactions."

And you can see the truth in Weishaupt's statement just by viewing the above names linked to Skull & Bones. The Illuminati is basically a tree with many branches. It passes on this "secret" knowledge to it's bloodlines and other initiates using secret societies like Knights Templar, Rosicrucians, Ku Klux Klan, Knights of Malta, Masonics, Skull and Bones, Jesuits, Thule Society (in which Hitler was a member of), Boule (the Black Skull & Bones), and Cap & Gown.

There are basically two types of these secret societies. There are ones in which the initiates are chosen (like Skull and Bones), and then there are ones like the Freemasons in which anyone can join and be a part of. The second of the two types of societies are structured in a way that when you join them, you don't realize what you are getting into. But through the initiation and satanic rituals (which we won't even get into), they filter out the less desirable and keep the wanted. And by the time you reach the upper echelon of these societies, you are "in too deep" and you can't get out even if you want to. And of course, those who tell any of the secrets are to be killed! That's why George GM James who was a Mason, was never heard from again after writing his book Stolen Legacy. That info wasn't supposed to be given out!

In his article, Masonry pt. 1: The Root of Global White Supremacy, M'Bwebe Aja Ishangi states that, *"Any mason who tries to tell you they're not devil worshipperz are either 1) lying to you because, again, they learn this starting with the 30th°; or 2) they are just like the undergrad fratz, a lower degreed mason who hasn't earned the right to know this secret yet."*

It's important to note that Masonry in and of itself is not evil. Knowledge is neutral. But what they do, as many of them are in allegiance with the Illuminati (namely Scottish Rite, York Rite, etc.) causes harm to our people.

Illuminati to the Hood

The members of these aforementioned secret societies will then go on to rule in secret, utilizing organizations like the Vatican, the Zionist Movement, the Council on Foreign relations, the Council on Foreign Affairs, the Trilateral Commission, the Bilderberg Group, The Committee of 300, The Royal Institute of International Affairs, The Club of Rome, The United Nations, and The Roundtable Group. And there power stretches down through the NSA, the FBI (which could mean the Federal Bureau of Investigation or Faith Based Initiatives), the CIA, and even health groups like Monsanto, the FDA, The AMA etc.

Through the Rothschild family, they also privately own the "non-federal" U.S. Federal Reserve Bank (as well as the federal banks of England, Germany, Italy, France, Canada, Australia, and Europe) and therefore influence all of the Governments decisions. These are all institutions that pull the strings (influencing and making political decisions in secret) of this "Matrix" that we live in. And yet, these are all institutions in which the masses can't vote in and out of office.

But it doesn't stop on the national level. This power also (directly and indirectly) stretches down through the entire political structure including, the U.S. Congress, the U.S. Senate down to the Local City Council, the U.S. Court system and even into the school system, where teachers will often have a tendency to tell young Black children, "You will never be anything in life."

We also see that through the Zionist Movement and the Council on Foreign relations, the entertainment and media industries are pretty much on lock down. Make

note that it was Edward Bronfman (member of Skull &
Bones) who financed the creation of gansta rap, which was
put out to counteract and silence the growing conscious
Hip Hop movement in the late 80's.

Even when you look in the streets, you will see that many of
the street gangs and/or biker gangs have Masonic and/or Skull
& Bones like initiations and symbolism that is associated
with them! This is deep, because originally gangs where
just cliques of people who got together (united) to hang out.
But, that by itself can become a threat to the establishment
when your objective is to keep those communities (especially
Black communities) under siege. Later on, gangs became a
destructive force. So now when a young Black youth wants
to join something... look what they are about to join!

We are dealing with a system that is so complex, that in
many cases, the people doing the bidding of the masters
don't even know who they are working for, and who
everything traces back to.

You see, insuring the war against unity in the Black
community is crucial to the power structure that is in
place. So anytime a Black person is seen or heard trying to
unify the people in the Black community for any reason,
one or several tools have to be activated to take action
against him/her.

But we never question what goes on, because the mass
media will only feed us a picture of the White people only

being benevolent and good. Consider how a lot of Black people are skeptical about doing business with Arabs. But have Arabs in this country done Black people worse than White people have? Or has our perception been manipulated?

The Illuminati rely on keeping the public fooled. And they succeed at this by using false representations on a host of things that affect what we perceive as reality.

Such as: Murdered Rapper Tupac Shakur gets a prison sentence for forcibly touching a woman's buttocks... though he had consensual sex with her. And the media directly gives the whole case the look of an undeniable forced rape conviction.

Or also consider Michael Jackson's memorial. While the whole world tuned in, on that very same day, the Pope was issuing a life-changing order. He called for all the governments of the world to initiate a "world political authority" to manage the global economy and for more government regulation of national economies to pull the world out of the current crisis.

And the mass media worked it very well. Ninety percent of the masses knew nothing about this.

Now, because of sensationalism, and our intensity for animation, oftentimes the truth gets hidden, and this is just a few of the ways how the Illuminati sell us on individuality and blindness. These tools were also used in perfect harmony in the 60's when the Peace/free-love movement permanently crippled our civil rights movement.

Now, divide and conquer under the design of individualism is a mainstay in the Black community. It explains the highly visible need for vanity. This is constantly corrupting the Black community.

This design alone makes it very easy to corrupt up & coming Black artists in the entertainment field. With the "hood" already set up for death, those with talent that scratch and claw their way out are met with forces that either trick, trap, or force the Black artist to propagate a negative perception of Blackness that does not allow prosperity for a group of Black people. This inserts an ugliness that nearly destroys the concept of unification, because the mind has been trained to think on an individual basis.

And if any of these artists decide to help their people unite and fight the very system that is immorally destroying them, those artists are met with severe consequences, depending on their impact in the black community.

Just look at the strange happenings that have taken place against Blacks with celebrity status:

Jimi Hendrix, Tupac Shakur, Jim Brown, Sam Cooke, Jam-Master Jay, Bob Marley, Malcolm X, Martin Luther

King, Huey P. Newton, Fred Hampton, Fred Hampton Jr., Assata Shakur, etc.

The list is endless. But this is not to be a gloom and doom session. You see, the biggest way that the Illuminati control the masses is not through force, but through their ability to influence the mind of the masses. They control what people think, and what they perceive.

That's why it would be good for us to turn off the Tell-lie-vision and radio, do some meditation and begin to free ourselves. We need to create our own media outlets so that we can propagate correct information, deprogram and then reprogram our own minds (and more importantly the minds of our children). We need to (before any moves are made) disconnect from the Matrix and move towards self reliance (which will take control of our destiny away from these controlled institutions).

But of course, there are some problems that we need to address that are keeping us from doing that very thing.

CHAPTER 3

THE DISCONNECT

Now that we have defined what the problem is, it is now time to move towards some solutions. But first, we must identify some things that are preventing us from reaching any type of solution. Most people believe that we struggle because we don't have any knowledge of our history or because we don't know who we are. But is that really true?

Here is the real truth. At this point, the scholarship is endless. We (or enough of us) know that we discovered civilization. We (or enough of us) know that we discovered the arts and sciences. We (or enough of us) know that we built the pyramids etc. A lot of White people even acknowledge it now. Now of course, many of us fight and debate over the "specifics" of what has happened in the past. And it's obvious that not all Black people are aware. But there are certainly enough to have started and ended a revolution by now. Yet, for all of our consciousness we haven't produced anything. We are still stuck. Why is that?

In this chapter we will discuss some mental blocks that are preventing us from coming together and working towards a common cause. These mental blocks are called:

Freek Philosophies

Freek Philosophy #1. Your Oppressor loves you and has your best intentions at heart.

If you were to take a survey and ask Black people, do they think that White Supremacist love them and want to do what's best for them, 99.9% of people out there would tell you emphatically NO! But we are here to claim that in Reality, 99.9% of people DO believe this (at least on a subconscious level), and we will state the case as to why.

Let's look at Hurricane Katrina. On August 29th, 2005, Hurricane Katrina passed through New Orleans. The Keyword in the last sentence is, "passed through." But suddenly, witnesses heard AND saw explosions going off right by the levy in the 9th ward. In the next couple of days New Orleans was almost completely flooded. The Government responded immediately. That's right... They responded immediately. FEMA was sent into Louisiana. They set up a check point between New Orleans and Greta Louisiana. People who tried to leave New Orleans were told they COULDN'T LEAVE. They were turned around and forced to go back to the Superdome where they were told they could get help. FEMA proceeded to lock them in the Superdome and watch them die! And, when people like the Red Cross tried to bring them help, FEMA held them back and would not allow them to bring in food and supplies!

A lot of the people who survived all of this are now dying a slow death in toxic trailers provided by none other than FEMA. But do you know what the worst part of this story is? Black people are actually running around and saying, "The Government failed us during Katrina" What?! Wait a minute. What does the word Fail mean? If you look up the word fail in the dictionary, you will get a definition like this.

> *Fail*
> 1. *To not achieve a particular goal. (The engine failed to start.)*
> 2. *To be negligent in one's duty. (The report fails to take into account all the mitigating factors.)*
> 3. *To cease to operate correctly. (After running five minutes, the engine failed.)*

When you say that the Government has failed, you are actually saying that the Government was trying to help us! The Government did not fail! The Government wasn't trying to help us; they were trying to kill us! And they succeeded!

> *Succeed*

1. *To obtain the object desired; to accomplish what is attempted or intended; to have a prosperous issue or termination; to be successful; as, he succeeded in his plans; his plans succeeded!*

Let us look at the Jena 6. Six teenagers charged with attempted murder after a school beat down? Once again, we still don't seem to understand. People were running around calling for the Federal Government to intervene on this system of injustice. You want the Federal Government to intervene on the system of injustice?!! Who created the system of injustice?

Listen. If your oppressor didn't want you to be oppressed, then he never would have oppressed you in the first place! We hate to be the bearer of bad news. But yes, those who are oppressing us, are actually trying to oppress us. They are not failing to make us the best we can be.

The justice system is not failing. It is succeeding. The justice system did not fail in the case of the Jena 6. The justice system didn't fail in the case of Sean Bell. The Justice system didn't fail in the case of Emmett Till or Medgar Evers. The JUST-US system didn't fail until O.J. Simpson got off! And if you don't believe us, go ask some White folks. They will tell you we're right.

You see, once you realize that the "system" is against you, then you have no choice but to either disconnect from it, or try to destroy it and create your own... BY ANY MEANS NECESSARY! But there is a faction of people who don't want us "thinking" like this, so they send out their people to unleash this trick psychology upon the masses.

At what point are we going to get a clue? We need to build our own rescue units. And when something like Katrina happens we should be ready. And if we have to go head up with FEMA, then so be it. Why is it that a race of people can enslave, torture, beat, kill us and cut off our genitals so that they can survive, yet, we can't fight for our own survival? And, if we had our Own Nation, we wouldn't have to worry about our own government throwing our babies in jail for going upside somebody's head. Why can't we understand this simple concept? Why of course, we are sitting around waiting for our oppressors to get it right (because after all, they are trying to help... but they are just failing). This philosophy is all apart of the Massa's plan.

Oh No... Don't go out and build your own liberation units. That would be crazy! Build your own Nation? Oh NO... That is a pipe dream!

But is it? I say, the only pipe dream is waiting on the Devil to save you from the Devil! That is a Freek Philosophy!

Freek Philosophy #2. We are our own worst enemy.

How many times have we heard the phrase, "We are our own worst enemy." used. The White man ain't doin nuthin to us. We are doing this to ourselves.

We as Black people are the only people on earth who blame ourselves for our own oppression. When you say that you are your own worst enemy, what are you really saying? If White supremacy is not involved in our day to day living, then why are we bringing up the rear here, and globally for that matter?

We have truly fell for the "illusion of inclusion" to the point that we think that there is actually a level playing field. This illusion is so strong that without analyzing what is going on, we have now began to "wonder" why we are in the position we are in.

The truth be told, there is nothing that goes on in the Black Community (whether it is gansta rap music, drug addicts, single family homes and so called Black on Black crime) that can not be traced back to White supremacy.

But why is this idea so important? If the "White man" is doing no more to us than anyone else, then we must be inferior! We are bringing up the rear in every category (except skin cancer) that you can think of. And we are doing this to ourselves? What is wrong with us? Are White people superior to us to the point that they just naturally excel and we naturally deteriorate?

You see, this "We are our own worse enemy" ideology causes us to have an inferiority complex. We talk all this mess about how great we used to be, but the truth is, we have little confidence, because we look at our condition and believe that we voluntarily put ourselves their. This is all apart of the Massa's plan. Massa stays behind the scene so as to make you feel that you are a product solely of your own doing.

Yes, we as Black people must take responsibility for our own actions, but we must not let the BEAST off the hook. We have to be balanced between the two. We need to study the "system" and understand what is being done to us in order to liberate ourselves.

But if you have bought into this falsified idea that White people left us completely alone after the Civil Rights Movement, and that we are here because of our own doing, then you will NEVER be free. You have just subscribed to a Freek Philosophy.

Freek Philosophy #3. Black Is Not Beautiful.

Of course at this point, we all know the deal. At the current time, the term "Black" is a negative term in this society, and the word "White" is a positive term.

At funerals you where Black.. and at weddings you where white. When you want to deny something you Blacklist it, and to allow something is to Whitelist it. Traditionally villains in the movies wore Black and the Hero's wore white. Black (according to the white, or so called white man) means death, and White means pure. It is very obvious why this is! It is definitely a psychological tactic used by a Europeans to create an inferiority complex amongst African people.

Unfortunately there are still factions of people among us who buy into this way of thinking. There are those who claim that we should not call ourselves Black because Black is bad (it's only an adjective), and we shouldn't call "them" white, because white is pure and we are giving them power.

Well, let's start with Black. Did our ancestors believe that black meant death? Or better yet, did they feel that it was just an adjective? Consider this. Where does the word Chemistry come from? The word comes from Khem (which means Black) and the suffix –istry, which means the study of. Chemistry is nothing more than the study of Black (the color). Why? Because simply put, Black is the Basis of life on earth. All life comes from darkness (Blackness). This word comes from Khemet (which is now called Egypt). Khemet is "The land of the Blacks!"

White people have declared the right to define, and now claim that Black is death. So rather than claim our right to define, we have to believe the European definition of this word because it's their language? We can't call ourselves Black, and we can't call them White?

Consider this. Is a European person white? No… but they are a hell of a lot closer to it than you are! Are you Black? No… But you are a hell of a lot closer to it than Europeans. So if white means "Pure" and Black means "Death," then if you are African (close to black skinned), then you are obviously inferior. How can you look in the mirror everyday and not have an inferiority complex when you think Black is death and White is pure?

We understand not calling yourself Black from a "legal" standpoint, but that is a different story. We as Black people, have to take back the right to define! Of course, most of us have… but, for those who haven't, you are subscribing to Freek Philosophy!

Freek Philosophy #4. Pro-Black Equals Anti White

This particular philosophy is one of the most powerful one available to Mr. Charley's disposal. Isn't it funny how other cultures are allowed to view their culture as superior to all others, yet when Black people do so, they are called racists?

Chinese people can get together and open up a "China Town." Now, of course you can go to Chinatown and shop till you drop. But if a Black person went into Chinatown and tried to stake some ownership in China Town, you would be looked at as a fool. The same thing goes for Little Tokyo etc. But if you build anything Black, and tell other races that they can't stake ownership, you are racist!

If a Jew believes that Black people have big genitalia because they are cursed, there is absolutely nothing wrong with it. As long as they don't "treat Black people badly," then what they believe is there own personal believe. But if a Black person believes that a white person is a recessive individual, then this person is racist!

It is perfectly okay for a White school system to teach your child that Columbus discovered America, Lincoln freed the slaves, that White people civilized the native indigenous people and also discovered math, science and art. But… if you tell your child that Black people were building pyramids while white people were practicing savagery, then you would of course be racist!

Millions of Black people are running like Super Mario from African history simply because we don't want to be racist.

It's no wonder we are bringing up the rear. It's no wonder we don't support our own. It's no wonder we will go and fight for someone else's kids, but won't fight for our own. It's no wonder our children have inferiority complexes. It's because we have subscribed to Freek philosophy.

Passive People

Remember the movements of the 60's and 70's? If you weren't alive at that time, you certainly know about or have heard about them by now. So by now you realize that these movements have died out, or in many cases are non existent at this point. But, why is that? What happened to the passion? Our ancestors were willing to give their lives (without a second thought) for what they believed in. But today, we seem to be willing to go along to get along. Instead of sitting around dumbfounded saying, "Well, we stopped what we were doing," we need to analyze and decipher what happened in order to be able to solve this problem.

There are of course a lot of things that factor into the way that we act now. One of them is that simply, we have been "punked." You see, all of our leaders (whatever venue they took) have been killed. And we can't seem to (or maybe we don't want to) deal with what really happened and who was involved in these situations. So because there has been no resolution, we as a people are scared (whether we will admit it or not). You see, when there is a serial killer on the loose who kills blonds and throws them into the river, all the women start dying their hair black! That is, until the killer is caught. Right now, there is a serial killer on the loose. And it doesn't matter what you do (whether you are an activist, a nationalist, a preacher or even a music artist). If you get too big and/or step too far out of line, you will be taken off of planet earth, and the people involved will go free! Until we deal with this problem (which often involves treason), we will forever be immobilized. You want to be the next Malcolm X? What happened to him?

Unity is also a big issue. If you look at all of the Black movements in the past, they have all been based on Black people unifying for a common cause, and against a common enemy. We seem to have lost this spirit. There are different reasons for this (some of which will be addressed in the "Reconstruction of Black Civilization Chapter"), but until we as a people learn to drop our differences, we won't see any success collectively.

Outside of all that has been mentioned in this chapter, we have to realize that there is a military strategy that is being used against us that is contributing to our disconnect. This strategy is health. Neely Fuller and Dr. Frances Welsing have already identified The 9 Areas of People Activity used by White supremacy as being (1) Economics, (2)Education, (3)Entertainment, (4)Labor, (5)Law, (6)Politics, (7)Religion, (8)Sex and (9)War. But there is now a new category that is emerging, which is (10)Health. In order to mount some type of revolution, one must be in a good state of health. This is mentally, physically and spiritually. Those in power realize this. So, there is a concerted effort to control the masses of people by attacking them with poisons. We will discuss these attacks in the next chapter.

CHAPTER 4

THE RECONSTRUCTION OF BLACK CIVILIZATION

Alright, we have now defined the problem, and we have also gone into some of the things that are keeping us away from making a move. But what is the ultimate solution? Well first, there is no "one" solution to our problem. There is no "one" specific game plan that is going to take us from where we are, to where we need to be. However, there are a few common denominators that we can put together to help us move in the correct direction.

Health Consciousness

Water Control pt 1. - Fluoride

I'm sure that we have all heard the expression, "There must be something in the water!" Well, at this point in time, no truer statement has been made.

Water is essential to life for us human beings. We drink it every single day. We cook with it every single day. And if you can deny the two previous statements (maybe you drink soda and eat fast food), you still take showers and bathe in water (which ultimately will lead to large amounts of it being absorbed into your body).

So it stands to reason, that if you can control the water supply of a mass of people, you have taken a big step in controlling the people.

With that being said, let's talk about a common ingredient that is in the water today. That ingredient is sodium fluoride. What is fluoride? Fluoride is any combination of elements containing the fluoride ion. In its elemental form, fluorine is a pale yellow, highly toxic and corrosive gas. In nature, fluorine is found combined with minerals as fluorides.

Now before we get into the issue of fluoride, let's sit back and let our minds go to work for a few minutes. Fluoride is said to be put into the drinking supply because it helps strengthen our teeth. This is very interesting. Now, let's pretend that this is true. There are a lot of ingredients that have been known to be beneficial to people.

Vitamin C has been known to be beneficial to many people! Vitamin C has been known to promote wound healing, promote younger looking skin and strengthen your immune system. It has been known to help people with asthma, allergies, high cholesterol, diabetes and cataracts. It is also a very powerful antioxidant. So... Why not dump it in the public drinking supply?

What about Vitamin D3? How about Omega 3 fatty acids? They have been known to protect against Cancer. What is the bigger problem, Cancer or Cavities? What about Green Tea? Nobody has overdosed on that right? We could go on all night.

Why would you dump any chemical (much less a heavy metal) into the public drinking supply? Why not just tell them how good it is and let them decide whether to consume it? You see, just being observant will let you know that something "fishy" is going on in the water. Now let's get into the history of man made fluoride.

During Adolf Hitler's reign in Germany in the 1930's, there where many experiments that were done on the people in Hitler's concentration camps (which is not to say that experiments aren't being done on people today). One of the most fruitful findings of the NAZI scientist was that by administering small amounts fluoride to a person, it would make that person become passive, stupefied and easy to rule over.

Before Germany invaded Poland, the German and Russian General Staffs met with each other to exchange military ideas. It was then that the Russians found out about fluoride and were given the idea to put small amounts of it into the drinking supply to control a mass of people.

Dictator Joseph Stalin found that by adding fluoride to the water supply at his prison camps that he could reduce his guards by **seventy five percent**! Nothing was ever reported on whether the prisoners had cavities or not.

Fluoride is also the main ingredient that is used in the making of the Atomic Bomb! Now of course, making these bombs causes a toxic waste. So... What better way to get rid of this waste than to sell it, and have it dumped into the water supply under the pretext that it is healthy for people?

Consider the following quote from a letter that Mr. Charles Perkins, a chemist sent to the Lee Foundation for Nutritional Research, Milwaukee Wisconsin, on October 2nd, 1954 (link to the full letter below).

> *"The real reason behind water fluoridation is not to benefit children's teeth. If this were the real reason there are many ways in which it could be done that are much easier, cheaper, and far more effective. The real purpose behind water fluoridation is to reduce the resistance of the masses to domination and control and loss of liberty."*

But what about your teeth? Well... here is a little truth on Fluoride.

Fluoride Deception part 1------------Fluoride Poisoning

Fluorine compounds or fluorides are listed by the US Agency for Toxic Substances and Disease Registry (ATSDR) as among the top 20 of 275 substances posing the most significant threat to human health. Fluorides, hydrogen fluoride and fluorine have been found in at least 130, 19, and 28 sites, respectively, of 1,334 National Priorities List sites identified by the Environmental Protection Agency (EPA). Consequently, under the provisions of the Superfund Act (1986), a compilation of information about fluorides, hydrogen fluoride and fluorine and their effects on health was required. This publication appeared in 1993.

http://www.tuberose.com/Fluoride.html

So if not good for your teeth, what is it good for?

- It causes skeletal and dental fluorosis (http://fluoridealert.org/issues/fluorosis/pictures/)
- It causes cancer
- It shortens life span
- It decreases fertility in males and females (it was used to make people sterile in the NAZI camps)
- It causes hypothyroidism
- It effeminizes men.
- It causes arthritis
- It takes 10-15 points off of your IQ.
- It accumulates in the pineal gland and calcifies it (cutting you off from the spiritual world). It also

causes disruptions in melatonin production, and it also can lead to early puberty in children.

- Also, by attacking your DNA repair enzyme activities can lead to full blown AIDS (or so called AIDS)!

What does fluoride have to do with our liberation? Health, plain and simple. You can't be a revolutionary if you are sick! And right now, the masses of people are sick, and also passive. Now, if you've been around for a while, you will notice that from generation to generation, we as a people have become more passive. The passion that existed 30-40 years ago is simply not there anymore and it is getting worse (as people continue to accept whatever goes on without a fight). Many people have even asked the question, "What happened?!" Well... Fluoride happened, and took effect over a period of time.

So to make a long story short, as long as people are consuming fluoride, there will be no revolution! There are many enemies of revolution. Fluoride is one of them.

And it's not just in the water. Below is a list of places you can get fluoride.

Here is some quick info on Fluoride (Sources and Detoxification).

The following are sources of fluoride

Cigarettes
Anti-Depressants
Anesthetics & Tranquilizers
Fluoridated Salt
Teflon Pans
Seafood
Boneless Chicken
Beer
Wine
Tea
Soda
Juice
Cereal
Infant Formula
Toothpaste

Removing Fluoride

The best way known to remove fluoride from your water is reverse osmosis. Regular water filters don't work, and in many cases, the bottled water that you may THINK is clean is nothing more than tap water or no better.

Reverse Osmosis (RO) is a filtration method that removes most types of large ions and molecules from water. Then the water is passed through a carbon filter to remove other chemicals that are left over. Often times, other stages are added to further filter the water. What is left is pure water and very few minerals.

You can get and purchase reverse osmosis water itself at some health food stores that have reverse osmosis machines (use glass carboys, or gallons if possible) that you can use, or you can have a reverse osmosis unit installed in your home. The later would probably be the best option as you absorb lots of water when you shower also. We wouldn't recommend buying bottled water from the grocery stores because the plastic leaches toxic chemicals into your water.

If you live in an apartment, you can also purchase shower filters that filter out chemicals also. Try to find one that filters out or neutralizes fluoride (they do exist).

As stated before, fluoride accumulates in the body and most notably it accumulates in the pineal gland and calcifies it! The following are some ingredients that have been known to assist in detoxifying from fluoride. These things can be purchased online or at health food stores.

Ingredients

Iodine: Supplementation has been clinically demonstrated to increase the urine irrigation of fluoride from the body. A great source of iodine is seaweed (kelp, which also can be used as a salt substitute).

Tamarind: The pulp, bark, and leaves from the tree can be converted to teas and strong tinctures, which have also shown the ability to eliminate fluorides through the urine. This tree is indigenous to Africa.

Boron: Boron has been known to remove fluoride from the body. Borax (which contains boron) has been shown success in detoxing from fluoride also. The prescribed usage is about 1/8 of a teaspoon along with a pinch of sea salt in a liter. This is to be consumed in small quantities every day.

Vitamin C: Vitamin C has been shown to assist in detoxing from fluoride and also decalcifying the pineal gland.

Calcium and Magnesium: Calcium is a mineral that attracts fluorides away from your teeth and bones and makes it easier to eliminate them. Magnesium is a mineral that inhibits the absorption of fluoride into your body. A good source is of course green leafy vegetables, or you can use a calcium/magnesium supplement.

Therapies

Dry Saunas: Dry Saunas combined with exercise release sodium fluoride stored in your fatty tissues. It can be intense enough to cause a healing crisis. So if you do this, keep the pure water intake high. You can also drink some chickweed tea to protect the kidneys while consuming green leafy vegetables (for calcium) or using a highly absorbable calcium and magnesium supplement.

Liver Cleanses: Liver Cleanses are considered effective for eliminating fluorides and other toxins.

Chealation Therapies: These include bentonite clay (internally or externally}, fulvic acid (NOT folic acid), DMSA, EDTA, cilantro pesto with chlorella etc.

NOTE: Another ingredient that is wonderful for decalcifying the pineal gland is **monatomic gold**.

References

http://www.naturalnews.com/026605 fluoride_fluorides_detox.html
http://www.tldp.com/issue/202/Notes_Fluorine.htm

Water Control pt 2. - Attack of The Gender Benders

The Cause

Continuing the theme of "It's in the water" we will now move on to another anti-revolutionary phenomenon. We have for a long time in the Black community talked about the emasculation and even the feminization of our men. This subject is always very important because the male is the protector of the family. If you can remove him from his place, then you can dictate the community.

Dr. Frances Welsing was quoted in The Isis Papers as stating the following:

"If the men of a people are oppressed, the women are brought under oppression - as they are dependent on their men for protection and defense. Women do not have the muscle mass to liberate a people or protect the young. Women develop the young, but their men must provide the protection and the security apparatus"

Those who are currently in power know the aforementioned to be true. They know that it will take Black men to step up and become warriors for our people in order for us to be free on a collective. That is why there is the move to destroy Black manhood in order to keep Black men subservient to "The Mann" and ruin their potential for aggressive challenge to White Supremacy.

Many tactics have been used and most have been covered, but one thing that is newer and rarely discussed is the attack of estrogen and estrogen mimicking hormones on society. This particular attack is not specific to the Black community but must be discussed.

We know that testosterone is the principal sex hormone in men whereas estrogen is the principal sex hormone in women. High levels of estrogen in a person will decrease their testosterone levels and vice versa. It has been shown that if you administer estrogen to male insects, that they will begin to develop female sex organs. So what better way to bend genders than to do the same to the male population?

Not only do we have an epidemic of fluoride in the water supply, but do to a lot of different factors, our drinking water has an excess of estrogen and estrogen mimicking chemicals in it and in our bodies. This phenomenon is caused by many different factors:

Industrial Farmed Meat and Dairy: Factory farms frequently dope up their meat with synthetic estrogen mimicking hormones to make them get big faster and produce more milk (in the case of cows).

Soy: As an alternative to meats, many vegetarians have turned to soy. Soy (especially genetically modified which most are at this point) is **extremely** estrogenic in the body.

Bisphenol A (BPA): Plastics contain BPA. BPA mimics the estrogen hormone in our bodies and can destroy a mans reproductive system. It is in the linings of plastics no. 3, 6, and 7 and it is also in the lining of canned foods. Other sources of BPA exposure include non metal dental fillings, infant formula (baby bottles), bottled water, newspaper ink, cashier receipts and most money!

Phthalates: Phthalates are also chemicals that mimic estrogen. They are found in artificial scents (deodorizers and air fresheners), pharmaceutical pills, paints, shower curtains, waxes, adhesives, children's toys and pretty much any soft plastic/vinyl product.

Parabens: These and other chemicals in personal products, detergents, dryer sheets, and cosmetics (make up, lotions, sunscreens, perfumes etc) contribute to estrogen dominance in men.

Birth Control: Birth control pills are a potent estrogen and they also increase risk of blood clotting, cancer and a whole list of ailments.

Others: Pesticides, herbicides, paints, solvents, car exhaust and chemtrails also promote estrogenic activity (as well as toxicity) in the human body.

The Effect

As a result of these chemicals (which are now showing up in our water supply), male fish are slowly becoming female fish (as well as hermaphrodites) and it is causing infertility amongst water based species and many of them are becoming extinct! So what do you think will happen when humans drink this water?

Well, it has been shown having an elevated level of estrogen in males will decrease muscle mass, increase feminine characteristics, and stunt growth in teenagers. It will also cause gynecomastia (breast enlargement), erectile dysfunction, impotence, premature ejaculation, low libido, chronic fatigue, excessive sweating and hot flashes. Now... Does that sound like a warrior to you? Or does it sound like a docile male who will do what he is told?

And this hormonal problem is not just about the males. Elevated estrogen in women are the cause of uterine fibroids, infertility, ovarian cysts, breast cancer, weight problems, endometriosis, bad circulation, amenorrhea (abnormal stoppage of menstruation) and male characteristics like body hair (mustaches etc).

Solutions

So what can you do about this? As in the case of fluoride, reverse osmosis is a good way to flush these excess hormones out of the water.

You will also want to consume organic fruits and vegetables to reduce your exposure to pesticides and fertilizers.

If you eat meat, you will want to purchase and consume organic and free range, hormone free meats. This will be more expensive. And that is of course why wealth consciousness is important.

Try to avoid plastic and plastic wrap when it comes to packaging food and water. Store your food and/or water in glass or stainless steel containers. And don't fall for the BPA-free okey doke. These plastics have shown to have many other estrogen promoting chemicals in them. Plastic is an enemy.

Use all natural detergent. Use Essential Oils rather than artificial scents. Use all natural cosmetics.

Use natural birth control rather than pharmaceutical pills (which are a major health hazard anyway).

There many natural alternatives to birth control pills:

Wild Yam, Queen Anne's Lace/Wild Carrot, Apricot Kernels, Neem Oil, Pomegranate, Rutin/Vitamin P, and Smartweed leaves to name a few.

Make sure you research the aforementioned methods thoroughly so that they are used correctly.

NOTE: Malt Liquors (such as Michelob, Hurricane, King Cobra, St. Ides, Old English etc.) which are predominantly sold in Black communities contain a military ingredient known as SaltPeter (or potassium nitrate) which plays a role in decreased sex drive and impotence. So if you are in the hood, you may want to avoid these.

Supplements

Now from the above list, you can see that it is almost impossible to completely avoid any of these estrogen-mimicking chemicals. Therefore we will present a number of substances known to flush out excess estrogen and also to keep it from metabolizing in your body:

Spirulina: Spirulina is a seaweed that is great at flushing BPA and other xenoestrogens out of your system. Chlorella is also a good supplement (as it is great in flushing out pesticides). Spirulina can be bought as a bulk powder or in tablet form from online or offline health food stores. These super foods are good for your overall health.

Mushrooms: Mushrooms (fungi) have been known to eat through xenoestrogens like BPA. The most commonly used is white button mushrooms for anti-estrogen purposes. But others are Shiitake, Maitake, Reishi, Cordyceps and Coriolus. These can be bought as a supplement or seasoning.

Folate: Preliminary studies have shown that folate can nullify and even reverse the effects of BPA and other xenoestrogens. Foods high in folate are: Black-eyed peas, Lentils, Okra, Broccoli, Iceberg lettuce, Beets, Lima beans, Sunflower seeds, Spinach, Brussels sprouts, Asparagus, Green peas, Cabbage, Avocados, Romaine lettuce, Tomatoes, Strawberries, Oranges, Bananas. You can also find folate as a supplement (though it is best utilized in food)

Stinging Nettle Root: Nettle root inhibits aromatase, which reduces conversion of testosterone and other androgens into estrogens. It is often used to treat prostate enlargement. It can be bought as a supplement.

Ginger Root and/or Turmeric: Both help to detoxify the liver & flush out excess estrogen. This can be used as seasoning, or a supplement.

Chamomile: Mostly consumed as a tea. It contains a natural aromatase (estrogen enzyme) inhibitor.

Kelp (seaweed): Kelp is often used as a salt substitute and is a good source of iodine and many other essential nutrients. Kelp has shown to have an anti-estrogenic effect. It can be bought as a supplement also.

You will also want to cleanse your liver, kidneys and your digestive tract to remove excess estrogen from your body. You can purchase liver/kidney cleanses online or at health food stores.

Fruits and vegetables on an empty stomach have been known to detoxify.

The following is a list of substances known to promote testosterone and can be purchased as a supplement:

Herbs: Tribulus Terrestris, Ashwaghanda, Sarsaparilla Root promote testosterone.

Vitamins and Minerals: Zinc, Selenium, Manganese, Vitamin D3, Vitamin C and B Vitamins promote and optimize testosterone levels.

General Health Recommendations

In this day and age, with all of the toxins out there, being health conscious really requires that one put in time to study health. But with that being said, if you follow these simple steps, your health will greatly improve.

- **Stay Away From Refined Foods:** Sugar is the no. 1 drug on the planet. Stay away from refined sugar, enriched (white) bread, enriched pasta, etc and move toward eating whole foods. Your body needs minerals to process and digest food. And since these grafted white foods have all of the minerals taken out of them, they actually leach minerals out of your body in order to process them. They are **ANTI**-nutritious. And fake sugars like Aspartame and Splenda (which destroy your brain cells) are no better! There are plenty of natural sweeteners out there like Stevia, Palm Sugar, Date Sugar etc.

- **Prepare Your Own Food:** Stay away from SickDonalds, Taco Hell, The Awful House, Die Hop, and "I Hope You Feel Lucky" Fried Chicken. And stay away from processed foods (TV dinners, Boxed foods, Canned Foods etc). Make time to prepare real food at your own home. If you are short on time, then you can always prepare your food in bulk, and eat leftovers for a period of time. And if you have to reheat, stay away from microwaves (as they change the molecular structure of your food and cause cancer).

- **Drink Plenty of Filtered Water:** Stay away from all of the toxic, acid Soda Pops (which drain the water out of your body), and Kool-Aids masquerading around as healthy water (like Gatorade, Vitamin Water etc.). You can add a ¼ - ½ of a teaspoon of all natural sea salt (Pink Himalayan, Celtic Sea Salt, etc) or some liquid trace minerals to a gallon of water to replace the minerals and electrolytes after you filter your water with reverse osmosis, or any filtering technique for that matter.

- **Get Proper Nutrition:** Stay away from synthetic multi-vitamins that you get from pharmacies. Synthetic man made vitamins are toxic. If you are going to go with a vitamin, then going with a whole food vitamin from a health food store (on or offline) is better. An even better idea is to supplement with super foods like Spirulina, Chlorella, etc. (which are not that expensive if you purchase them in bulk).

- **Buy Organic:** Whatever type food you eat, organic is better. So as much as possible, stay away from genetically modified fruits and vegetables (which are sprayed with hormone laden pesticides) and hormone laden meats. Finding food that is not genetically modified these days can be a chore. A great resource to help in that area is

the Non GMO Shopping Guide (http://www.
nongmoshoppingguide.com/download.html)

Unity

It has been said for as long as anyone can remember that
Black people need to "unite." As a matter of fact, it has
been said so much, that it is almost played out. Most
Black people have become desensitized to the concept of
"uniting" and that is too bad.

But even more importantly, on a subconscious level, many
Blacks are afraid to try to unite. This is because; they
believe that the beast has all the weapons and would just
kill everybody. Well, to all of the grasshopper minded
Negroes among us, you may want to consider the
following information.

One Scared and the Other One Glad of It

In 1978, the National Security Council Memorandum
#46 was signed into law in the U.S. This document
basically states that The U.S. Government must monitor
and launch covert and clandestine groups to stop Black
people in the world from uniting together. This way the
U.S. can continue to drain South Africa of its natural
resources.

The document also states that there should be mistrust created in America towards Blacks who want to unite, and that it also should be, "borne in mind that black Africa is an integral part of a continent where tribal and regional discord, economic backwardness, inadequate infrastructures, drought, and famine, are constant features of the scene."

With this mentality in place, genocide forced upon Africans will be viewed as "no big deal" even by Blacks in America. And a lot less ruckus will be raised about America's conquest of raw materials there.

You see, even though "Black People Uniting" has played out amongst a lot of Black people, it has never played out with regard to White Supremacy trying to stop it.

But why is this? Let's go back to old school slavery. If a slave master had a plantation, his first priority was to keep those slaves from coming together against him. Many tactics would be used to accomplish this. Some of those tactics would include having his castrated house Negro monitor and spy on the field Negroes, taking away their drums, torturing and/or sodomizing the strongest Afrikan while everyone on the plantation watched, separating families etc.

Now, why would the big bad slave master (with all the guns) go through all of this trouble to keep slaves from uniting? Because the slave master was afraid of the slaves!

If the slaves ever united and came against him, the game was over. Now maybe since he had guns he could kill all of them. But guess what. No Slaves, No Plantation. If a slave master kills ALL of his slaves, then he is out of business! You can't have slavery without slaves.

So of course, he would have to make an example out of those few Negroes that stepped out of line (like the Martin Luther King's, the Malcolm X's, the Khalid Muhammad's of those days) to keep the rest of the slaves scared. So the bottom line is, in order for the slave master to maintain control, he had to keep his slaves in a mental state of fear by creating the illusion that he had all the power when in fact, he had none.

This is why you have things like guns, drugs and liquor being circulated specifically in the Black communities, FBI Cointelpro, the Boule etc. This is why the government is moving toward monitoring the masses of people (national ID cards and microchips scheduled to be planted in human bodies etc) and National Security Memorandums. The Rulers are afraid! If they weren't, then they would come out in a press conference and say, "**We are running this show, and if you Negroes don't like it, then raise up!**"

They know better than to do this. That's why they always use covert and clandestine tactics. This is the classic game of, "One is scared and the other one glad of it." They are afraid of us, and we are afraid of them. These tactics are being used effectively today and that is one of the reasons Black people are so afraid. Therefore, we need to drop the

"One Messiah" model and play team ball. Come together and have everyone do their part.

As strong as the beast is, his strength is based on illusion. And as powerless as we seem, that is based on illusion also. And this illusion has to stay alive because there is nothing scarier than fighting against an enemy that you can only defeat if you can convince them that it's not worth fighting. The statement that, "Racism is born out of fear" is simple, yet profound.

Right here in America, Black people are the #1 consumer (and the VAST majority of that goes to white corporations). If Black people began to unite and spend that money with our own people, it would shut down "their" economy very quickly. And if Black people united on a global scale, it would shut down White Supremacy almost instantly. The system of White Supremacy can't and never has been able to survive without the theft of labor, knowledge, wealth and resources from Afrika and those of Afrikan descent.

The Protocol of the Movement

Okay, so let's all just unite! Right? Well this is of course, easier said than done. Especially considering all that has been put in place just to keep us from doing so. And let's not kid ourselves; it's not going to happen overnight.

However, inside GroupThink (located at <u>Destee.com</u>), a goal was set and attained. We decided that we were going to come together and write a book for the liberation of our people and for the support of Destee. And we would accomplish this By Any Means Necessary (B.A.M.N.) After a long journey, and using the protocol that is about to be expressed, three Black men with diverse points of view (who to this day, have never once met each other) were able to unite and put together this entire book.

What resulted was this very work, which we believe enriches the conscious Afrikan mind with key points of vision that provide insight into the trickery that keeps us divided and renders us helpless. And we also believe that it gives us the tools and ammunition to protect ourselves and begin the process of our liberation.

Now, there are thousands of reasons (excuses) that could have kept us from uniting. So it seems logical that in order to unite, we had to destroy the reasons. So in order for us to be able to put aside our differences and come together, there had to be a protocol (mechanisms) in place to help us do so.

In one of Groupthink's early meetings, a religious topic was brought to the table. What ensued was a religious debate that lasted for hours. But there was no conclusion. From this meeting, the idea came about that there were some things that just need not be discussed during our meetings in order for us to be productive. These things were:

1. Religion
2. Barack Obama

3. Matriarchal vs. Patriarchal issues
4. Meat Eaters vs. Vegetarians

Our intent was not to get anyone to give up or even hide their beliefs. We promote these debates and discussions. However, during business hours (the time that we come together to problem solve) certain issues would not hit the table because they would only cause disputes. If a person does venture into one of these topics, they will be called on it. And if they can't handle that rule, then they can't participate.

Just like when/if you have a job. During your job, you don't run up on people with your beliefs because if you did, you could be fired. And for those of us who call ourselves revolutionaries, it is our "JOB" to work together to provide solutions for our people. Even if it means coming together with those who we don't see eye to eye with, or sometimes even like.

Interestingly enough, once we removed the above topics from the table, everything ran smoothly. We agreed on virtually everything. There was little to no friction between us. Once we began to focus on our common enemy, everything fell into place.

One must realize that the issues that we often fight over are not the only things that need to be resolved to solve our problem; because if they were, the people who got it "right" would have solved the problem by now.

Right now, we as Black people are at the stage of discovering new things, and piecing together our history. Some are further along than others. There are some things that we as a people are nowhere near coming to a conclusion on. Debates on these topics are often never ending. And frankly, we don't have that kind of time.

Keep in mind that there are a lot of Non-Black people, groups and religious organizations out here that have differences with each other (even the elite). But when it comes time to determine the status of Black folk, they all come together instantaneously and keep us at the bottom. Why can't we come together for our own liberation?

We feel that the above protocol can be a prototype for people and organizations all over the world to get together and unite. The current list (of topics not to hit the table) is not set in stone. It can vary from group to group.

If a subject matter comes about that divides the group and that division will keep the group from moving forward, then it has to be resolved through consensus based resolution. But if a subject matter divides the group, and the group can move forward and function without resolving the debate, then that topic will be added to the list. This is something that has to be analyzed in the case of disagreements.

Now, just like in the case of The GroupThink Project Assembly, there will be those who will not be willing to drop differences. That's fine. Wish them the best. But they can't be a part of the group. As revolutionaries, we need to liberate our people. Even if it means dropping our differences, and coming together with people who we don't agree with, don't like and can't stand. By ANY Means Necessary! Our revolution will happen whether we like it or not. Will you be in on it?

Wealth Consciousness

It doesn't matter what you want to do. If you want to build a revolutionary army, it takes money. If you want to go back to Africa and set up shop, it will take money. If you want to open a school, it will take money. If you want to do a food project and start growing your own food, it will take money. If you want to survive, it takes money! Any move that we as a people want to make (individually or collectively) will take money. We live in a capitalistic society. And whether or not you think that is right or wrong, that is the way it is. How can you give to your community if you don't have any money? How can you help your fellow man or woman if you can barely get by yourself? How can we as a people unify and put together projects toward empowering our people if our last $50 is going towards paying off that last bill?

Most people would agree that buying organic food from a health food store would be better for one's health than eating Ramen Noodles and Hamburger Helper (along with hormone laden ground beef). This is why there is a tight economic squeeze going on in the planet. The Illuminati know that eating garbage will keep us sick and docile and unable to mount any type of liberation movement. This is the reality. So we need to learn to attract money.

Unfortunately, we in the Black community often have an aversion to the very thing that we need to survive! We have been trained to believe that money is evil. If somebody has too much of it, they must have sold out. Only House Negroes and White Supremacists are supposed to be rich. Revolutionaries have to struggle, give away their material for little or nothing, and live off of donations. Many movements in the past have failed because of this ideology.

The Beast has guns, missiles, trained assassins, armies, weather machines and well to do House Negroes in their corner. You can't beat that with, "**Let's everybody put $5.00 in the pot**" money. We have to be real with ourselves and understand the world that we are living in. So if Black people want to succeed at doing anything at all, we are going to need money, and lots of it! We are going to need some "Rich Revolutionaries" and some "Conscious Ballers" to achieve what we need to.

We need to begin to think and grow rich. We need to become entrepreneurs! We need to learn how to build wealth. And there are many resources out there to help us do that. And we can't shy away from things like "The Secret" and "Law of Attraction" because it is a stolen legacy.

Again, we live in a system of capitalism (globally). That system is not about to change anytime soon. You can move to whatever country you want to, but you are still ultimately ruled by a system of capitalism. They don't call it **Global** White Supremacy for no reason. So going somewhere else is not going to solve the problem. In order for us to win this game, we will need a consolidated effort (mentally, physically and spiritually).

Wealth is at the heart of nationalism. This is why they burned down Black Wall Street. You can't say that you are against wealth and opportunity, yet simultaneously say that you are a nationalist. That is an oxymoron because nationalism is about wealth in the community (which includes "the collective" and "the individual"). Black Power with no resources to back it up is useless. This is the reason that we haven't gone anywhere thus far. And in order to neutralize the military strategy that is being used against us, it will take money. Wealth is the final frontier to be conquered. So we are going to have to pull our heads out of our behinds on this one.

You would be hard pressed to say that our ancestors after 400 years of being worked to death (outside of being raped, tortured and murdered) to provide White people with wealth and riches would delight in seeing their descendents resign to a state of struggle; especially considering the fact that we spend almost a trillion dollars every year (most of which goes directly in the pocket of those who we claim are our oppressors).

This is not about "flossing" in front of the masses of Black people while being subservient to Whites (we've got plenty of million dollar slaves out there). This is about using money as a tool for our advancement. As crazy as it may sound, if you truly believe in the liberating of our people, then you have to be willing to do it By Any Means Necessary, even if it means building wealth.

Empowerment Experiment (formerly the Ebony Experiment)

Their project, the **Empowerment Experiment** –formerly the Ebony Experiment — grew from their desire to spread awareness about black businesses that provided high quality, economical merchandise and to dispel the myth held in black communities that black products and services are inferior to those sold by other ethnicities.

You see, the Andersons made a public choice to spend all of their money with black business owners and professionals or black manufactured products throughout the entire year of 2009. They estimate that they spent about 70% of their income or about $70,000 on black businesses last year. They got the idea from similar projects like the "**No Impact**" family, who lived a year without electricity to reduce their carbon footprint.

They also wanted to draw a parallel between the lack of black businesses and the high rates of unemployment, recidivism, and chronic illness in black communities, says John Anderson, 38, a financial consultant with AXA Advisors, and president of **In Sight Financial Management**, his own consultancy firm.

Though the experiment is over, their cause is unfinished. The goal of EE was never to connect to the mainstream, but to encourage black people to support black-owned businesses, says Maggie, also 38 and a stay-at-home mother of two with a law degree and an MBA from the University of Chicago.

They plan to re-launch their Web site to include a directory of black businesses nationwide, a ticker that will track the money spent at black companies, and allow users to rate the products and services listed on their site. Researchers at Northwestern University's Kellogg Graduate School of Management will release a study on the experiment this spring. Finally, by June the Andersons hope to publish a book chronicling their experience and the findings of the study.

Article written by Marcia Wade Talbert, **BLACK ENTERPRISE**
http://www.blackenterprise.com/2010/01/12/andersons-complete-year-of-buying-black/

CHAPTER 5

CONTRIBUTING AUTHORS COMMENTARY

Uniquely, this Chapter of the book, the *Contributing Authors Commentary* section, allows free-style composition that rivals literary freedoms enjoyed by authors of typical prose. The three contributing authors exercise personal mannerisms, designed to shock the reader into a process of self solution. This section allows departure from GT's group consensus prototype, by which readers may be able to recognize the consortium effect of the work.

And just as unique is the manner in which the authors proceeded about their work and reached consensus on the material in the book. Individuals from different backgrounds came together online, having never met personally, and were able to establish rapport without prejudice and see eye to eye without conflict.

What's More Important to You.........WARRIOR
Your Religion or your Blackness?
BELIEVING IN THE WHITE MAN........WARRIOR
A Mass Murderer Named Progress.....By the Brown H0rnet
Racism, the Final Frontier.................Clyde C. Coger, Jr.

WHAT'S MORE IMPORTANT TO YOU...YOUR RELIGION OR YOUR BLACKNESS?

By *Warrior*

THERES ALWAYS GONNA BE DIFFERENCES WITHIN OUR PEOPLE.......NO MATTER WHAT THE SITUATION IS...HISTORICALLY, THE EUROPEAN DID A HELLUVA JOB DIVIDING US......I'M FULLY AWARE OF THAT......I WITNESS IT & I LIVE WITH IT EVERYDAY....

I FIGHT WHITE RACIST PEOPLE AND THEIR TWISTED RULES AND THEIR WICKED GAMES EVERYDAY......EVERY DOGGONE DAY

THE CIVIL RIGHTS VICTORIES & ITS DEMISE GAVE US A SERIOUS LOOK AT HOW WELL THE EUROPEAN CAN DIVIDE US.......DESPITE THE OBVIOUS CRUELTY THAT WE KNEW

BEFOREHAND.....AND WHAT WE KNOW FIRSTHAND......

THEY ARE ALWAYS USING THE WORD "WE" AS IN "ALL OF US FROM ALL COLORS AND CREEDS", THE VERY MINUTE THE BLACKMAN POINTS OUT A LEGITIMATE WRONG-DOING ON THE WHITE MAN'S PART....

THE WAY THEY USE "WE" IS AT THE CORE OF THEIR DIVISIVE TACTICTS....INCLUDING RELIGION....AND I'M SICK OF BLACK FOLKS BUYING INTO THAT MESS.....BECAUSE ALL IT DOES IS SUSTAIN THEIR RACIST PRACTICES.....

BUT THERE'S AN ISSUE I HAVE.....AND I WANNA KNOW SOMETHING....NOW, BEFORE I ASK THIS QUESTION.....I WANNA SAY THIS.....

YOUR HOME, BATHROOM, LAND, CARS, CLOTHES, JEWELRY, YOUR THOUGHTS,....... AND........YOUR RELIGION.........IS YOURS.....AND YOURS ALONE...UNLESS A PERSON CHOOSES TO SHARE THEM WITH ME, I HAVE NO BUSINESS WHATSOEVER, ATTENDING TO THEM......... YANNO?? BECAUSE ITS THEIRS.....BESIDES, I DON'T WANT NOBODY ATTENDING TO MINE....

NOW.....BLACKNESS......THAT RIGHT THERE.... BELONGS TO EACH AND EVERY ONE OF

US....WE HAVE FULL RIGHTS TO CONFRONT ONE ANOTHER ON THAT....THAT BUSINESS BELONGS TO ALL OF US....

THERE'S BLACKNESS AT THE ORIGIN IN NEARLY EVERYTHING WE KNOW......RIGHT NOW......AND ITS UNDISPUTABLE....THOUGH IT HAS BEEN MISREPRESENTED, MISGUIDED, & MISTAKENLY GRAVITATED......AMONG MANY OTHER NEGATIVE THINGS...

NOW.....WITH THAT SAID.....MY QUESTION IS : WHAT COMES FIRST, YOUR RELIGIOUS BELIEFS OR YOUR BLACKNESS???

THATS A HELLUVA CHOICE.....BECAUSE I CAN GO TO THE BIBLE AND STAND ON DEUTERONOMY 28 ALL DAY EVERYDAY........AND NO ONE CAN KNOCK ME DOWN....NO MATTER WHAT ANY OF THEM SAY.....AND SUPPOSEDLY PROVE.....

BUT THATS NOT MY CONCERN, NOR IS IT MY CHOICE........TO BE HONEST, I CONSIDER IT MY SACRIFICE....BECAUSE MY GOD SAYS TO CONSIDER FAITH IN HIM 1ST, OBEY HIS LAWS 2ND, & UNITE MY PEOPLE 3RD.....AND DUETERONOMY 28 TELLS ME EXACTLY WHO THOSE PEOPLE ARE.....

BUT.....I CONSIDER MY BLACKNESS FIRST..... MOSTLY BECAUSE....I'M READY TO GET DOWN.....

FOR MYSELF....MY FAMILY.....MY COMMUNITY, AND MY PEOPLE....WHAT SAY YOU??

BELIEVING IN THE WHITE MAN

By *Warrior*

JUST CONSIDER WHAT WE ALREADY KNOW.....

WE (BLACK PEOPLE FROM THE TRANS-ATLANTIC SLAVE-TRADE) HAVE SUFFERED TREMENDOUSLY FOR WHAT HISTORY TELL US.......FOR CENTURIES.

WE SUFFERED AT THE HANDS OF OUR OWN (EGYPT)...
WE SUFFERED AT THE HANDS OF THE ARABS....
THE PORTUGESSE....
THE EUROPEAN......AND SO ON...

THOSE OF US WHO ARE BIBLE-BELIEVERS HAVE GREAT FAITH THAT THE PROMISE FROM OUR GOD, YAHWEH, TO ABRAHAM WILL DELIVER US, IF WE OBEY AND PRAY....

AND, THROUGH THE COURSE OF OUR BLINDNESS WITHIN OUR MANY PUNISHMENTS, OUR SUFFERING COULD NOT BE CLEARER....

OF ALL THE YEARS OF SLAVERY WE HAVE KNOWN, IT'S THE WHITE MAN WHO HAS DONE THE MOST DAMAGE TO US....

HE HAS DIVIDED US SO PERFECTLY, THAT WE NOT ONLY BELIEVE WE ARE FREE WITHIN HIS SYSTEM OF LIVING, A HEALTHY NUMBER OF US CAN ONLY SEE OUR INDEPENDENCE, WITH ONLY HIS HELP, UNDER HIS RULERSHIP.....

WE ALL WORK FOR HIM...
WE ALL GIVE HIM OUR WAGES TO MAKE HIM
     STRONGER...
WE ALL EMBRACE HIS STYLE OF
     ENTERTAINMENT...
WE ALL USE HIS DEFINITION OF
     ACCEPTANCE FOR SUCCESS...
WE ALL LOOK FOR HIS APPROVAL....ABOVE
     OUR OWN...
WE ALL FIGHT EACH OTHER WITH THE
     TOOLS HE GIVES US...
WE ALL USE HIS LOGIC FOR PERSONAL GAIN
     & SURVIVAL....

AND AFTER EVERYTHING HISTORY HAS TAUGHT US, WE STILL CONTINUE TO SUPPORT DIVISION, SELFISHNESS, & HIS IDEA OF PERSONAL SACRIFICE OVER THE SEEMINGLY UNATTAINABLE......UNITY

CONSIDERING THAT THE BLACK WOMAN IS OUR FIRST & ORIGINAL TEACHER, CAPTIVITY SHOULD ANGER HER TO EMPOWER US AS CHILDREN TO PREPARE FOR WAR....

BUT SOME OF OUR WOMEN HAVE DEEPLY ACCEPTED OUR CAPTIVITY, AND LOVE FOR OUR WELL-BEING HAS EXCUSED HER FROM FEAR OF LOSS...

AND WE GROW UP WITH A CERTAIN BOND OF ADMIRATION FOR THE WHITE MAN, WITH FULL KNOWLEDGE OF HIS EVIL TRICKERY ON OUR PEOPLE....

WE RUSH QUICKLY FOR HIS FRIENDSHIP AND HIS GUIDANCE....AND WILL FIGHT ON OUR KNEES AGAINST OUR OWN......JUST TO MAINTAIN WITHIN HIS ORDER..

EVEN WHILE DIVIDED, THE PASSION FOR VANITY IS MORE IMPORTANT THAN A UNITED EFFORT FOR AN IDEA....THAT BENEFITS EVEN TWO OF US, DIVIDED, IN THE SAME DWELLING....

THE PROFOUND MISTAKE WE MADE WAS TO BEGIN TO BELIEVE IN HIM, AND THEIR GOVERNMENT, RATHER THAN IN OURSELVES........AND WE HAVE SUFFERED

FROM THAT MORE......THAN WE SUFFERED FROM SEGREGATION.

DR. SHELBY STEELE

THE IMPLEMENTATION OF AMERICAN-EUROPEANISM HAS FILTERED THROUGH US REPEATEDLY & THOROUGHLY, LEAVING BEHIND SO MANY BROKEN PIECES, MAKING IT IMPOSSIBLE TO CLEANSE OURSELVES OF THE SMALLEST PARTICLES THAT CLING TO OUR SOULS DESPERATELY....

IT SHOULD BE THEM LOOKING FOR OUR ACCEPTANCE....AND NOT THE OTHER WAY AROUND...

HE CAN AFFORD TO LET US KNOW THE TRUTH NOW, BECAUSE HIS MORALS, THAT ARE AMPLIFIED THROUGH TELEVISION, HAVE CEMENTED HIS IDEA, AND HIS PERSPECTIVE, OF DIVISIONS IN THE BLACK RACE....

I SAY THIS TO THOSE OF YOU THAT BELIEVE IN THE WHITE MAN, EXCUSE HIM OF HIS OPPRESSION AGAINST US, AND SUPPORT HIS WAYS.....

AND ALSO....TO THOSE OF YOU THAT FOLLOW HIM, IN HIS SECRET SOCIETY FOUNDATIONS,

THAT HE STOLE FROM THE AFRICAN AND CHANGED TO FIT HIS IDEA OF POWER....

YOUR NUMBERS, THOUGH THEY DO NOT MATTER...ARE DECLINING....

THE HOUSE NI**ER, THE SELL-OUT, & THE LEARNED FOOL WILL NOT PREVAIL..

WARRIOR (PointMan)

Bio:

CURRENTLY AN AUTO MANUFACTURING WORKER
HIGH SCHOOL GRADUATE
3 YEARS OF COLLEGE....IN JOURNALISM & SPEECH
4 YEAR VETERAN OF U.S. AIR FORCE...
ACTIVIST FOR THE EQUALITY OF BLACK PEOPLE
FATHER OF FOUR DAUGHTERS..
PROUD SON OF BAPTIST MINISTER..

A Mass Murderer Named Progress

Integration or Disintegration?

By **The Brown H0rnet**

The scene starts at the **Lilly White Model Magazine Inc** headquarters. **Charlie**, the C.E.O. of the magazine sits across the table from **Cecil Mann** and begins to discuss his ailing business.

Charlie: Mr. Mann, I just don't know what to do! I've tried everything that I know. More advertising, lower prices... but my magazine's revenue continues to plummet!

Cecil: I'm completely aware of your situation.

Charlie: And I tell ya, that frickin **Nubian Model Mag**... Their business goes UP every year! **They are even taking some of our customers**! I mean, what's the deal? What do they have that we don't?

I mean take a look at this magazine! Have you seen these photos? My Goodness... This woman's buttocks is almost running off the side of the page!! This is ridiculous. And Afro Puffs?

Cecil: D**N... she IS hot!

Charlie: You're not helping!

Cecil: (chuckles) Listen Charlie. I've seen your situation many times before. There's nothing for you to worry about. I've already set up a phone appointment between you and Mr. **Alex RockFeather**. This is his number. He is expecting your call.

Charlie: Who is Alex RockFeather?

Cecil: He is the president of the RockFeather Advertising Agency for the Promotion of Equality (**R.A.A.P.E.**)

Charlie: I want profits! I'm not interested in Equality!

Cecil: You will be. Go ahead and call the number.

(phone rings)

Charlie: Hello? Yes Mr. RockFeather. I'm Charlie and.... oh, you already know then. Yes, I'm struggling man. You are a highly recommended person, so what are your suggestions?

(listens)....

Wha... What?! Are you crazy? How in the hell would THAT help raise profits? Are you trying to put me out of business and discredit my name?! And besides how do you expect me to get their attention? They have their OWN agenda!

Wha... WHAT?! You mean **those people WORK FOR YOU?!** BAHHHAAAA HA HA HAAAA! Am I on candid camera or something? Mr. Mann, are you sure you didn't give me the wrong number?

Cecil: (laughing) yes, I'm sure.

Charlie: Ok mister RockFeather. I'm desperate and I'll probably be out of business in 2 years anyway. So tell you what. I'll give your little cockamamie scheme a shot. And if it works like you say it will, I'll gladly pay you. Alright... bye bye. (hangs up)

HA!!! Mr. Mann, this better not be a joke.

Cecil: Well, my job is finished. I've got to be going now.

Charlie: Alright, I'll see you later.

Cecil: And by the way... Can I borrow that magazine?

---

1 week later

Broadcasting from Wolfe News

Sarah: Good Evening and welcome to the **Wolfe Network** (the source you can trust for unbiased reporting)... Today on the 5 o'clock news, a new terrorist threat has been found, 2 people got shot in the hood and a little white girl is missing... But FIRST... The scene at Lilly White Model Magazine, the historically European Magazine is one of unexpected chaos. What's going on down there Bill?

Bill: Well Sarah... It's kind of crazy out here. Right now, the **CNA (Council on Negro Affairs)** is outside having a protest. It's pretty wild out here and the police are monitoring the situation, but so far, no one has gotten hurt. Right now, I'm just trying to get someone that I can talk to... oh.. hang on, here we go. Yes... sir, what is going on with this protest today?

Negro: We are sick and tired of Lilly White magazine, not recognizing Black Beauty. This magazine has been in business for 55 years and not ONE BLACK MODEL? We are here today to SHOW the people that we refuse to give anyone "OUR" business who doesn't represent us. It's time for Lilly White to step up to the plate and stop discriminating against us!

Bill: Well... there you have it. The Council on Negro Affairs is making their voice heard and **pushing towards equality** for there people as always. Back to you Sarah.

---

2 days later

Shawn: Hello and welcome to the **Shawn Show** on The Wolfe Network. I'm your host, **Shawn (O'Really?)**.

Today on the show... **"Is Lilly White Too White?"** Today I have a couple of powerful and controversial guests on the show to duke it out. First, we have a representative of the CNA, Mr. **Thomas Ad'Visor**. He does diligent work in the Black community and strives for the upliftment of his people.

It's good to have you on the show again Thomas! You look a little exhausted Thomas. You doin ok?

Thomas: I do apologize Mr. (O'Really?). I just witnessed the birth of my twin niece and nephew. I kind of lost track of time and had to hurry here.

Shawn: That's beautiful Thomas. So listen, before we get started, tell us about your new organization. Now how do you pronounce this... is it Mildew?

Thomas: Yes, it's pronounced Mildew because it's easy to remember. It stands for the **Multicultural-Negros Integration League that Dreams of being Equal with Whites**. The N is silent.

Black Radical: Yeah... it always is.

Shawn: (sighs)... and ladies and gentlemen as you can see, we have another guest on the show... **Black Radical**. He is a Black Nationalist. He does... some things in the community too, I guess. Well... Black... it's good to have you on the show.

Black Radical: Don't even front Shawn.

Thomas: Now see… that's what I mean! How can we ever be **equal with White people** (The Ultimate Orgasmic Experience) when people like you run around being unprofessional and using Ebonics all the time. This is National TV! We will never be respected by our White counterparts with you around.

Black Radical: Trick… Do you even believe half the nonsense that comes out of yo mouf?! How much does da Man pay you? Or maybe what they say is true. **Breathing in Mildew causes mental illness**.

Shawn: STOP RIGHT THERE BLACK! Now I will not have you being disrespectful on my show! Now… The Topic of the show today is "Is Lilly White too White?" So Mr. Radical what do you think of the latest issue of Lilly White Magazine?

Black Radical: I saw the cover of it. It was aight.

Shawn: But… but… aren't you offended by Lilly White Magazine being around for 55 years and never recognizing Black beauty?

Black Radical: Hell, I don't read Lilly White Magazine, so it aint really my concern.

Thomas: Are you crazy? Lilly White has been around for 55 years and has never had one Black Model and that doesn't even bother you? Well I for one am very concerned. I've had my eye on Lilly White for some years now. And I would like to see a Sister being represented.

Black Radical: Well if you want to see a Sista being represented then why don't you **GO AND BUY A BLACK MAGAZINE**?! Like the Nubian Model Mag... did you see **Tonya** rockin the Afro Puffs last week? Lawd Have Mercay! Booty d**n near off the page! She must be rubbin steroid creams on that...

Shawn: BLACK!!!

Black Radical: Ok,.. I'm sorry.. I just got a little carried away. But for real. Why would I be concerned wit tryin to get a Sista in Lilly White which I don't even read? They have their magazine, we have ours. **That's EQUALITY!**

Thomas: (loud gasp)

Shawn: What? But **ISN'T THAT SEGREGATION?!**

Thomas: (choking and hyperventilating)

Shawn: Isn't that what your grandparents fought so hard against? Didn't they dedicate their lives to strive for equality?

Black Radical: First of all, slow your roll... you don't know my grandparents, and second. IS **CHINATOWN**

SEGREGATION? IS **LITTLE TOKYO** SEGREGATION? Why is it that every body else can have their own c..........

Shawn: Uh... um. Oops. Ladies and Gentleman it seems that we have lost Black Radical. I guess we had a bad connection. So Thomas, what are your thoughts on this?

Thomas: (taking deep breaths). I'm sorry Shawn... just give me a second. Radical shook me up a little.

Shawn: Take your time Thomas

Thomas: Ok... Shawn you are SO right. I couldn't have said what you said any better. We have fought for years to achieve equality. And we have made a lot of "**PROGRESS**" and we are not ABOUT to let an uneducated, ignorant FOOL undermine all that we have worked for!

Shawn: Yes, I did break it down nicely didn't I. I've learned ho... oops, well ok. But Thomas. What about Mr. Charlie's explanation? He says that Lilly White is a traditionally European magazine. He says that he is not against Blacks, it's just not a Black Magazine.

Thomas: Not against Blacks huh. Yeah, I've heard that before. The bottom line is, that Lilly White needs to get with the times! They are only hurting themselves! By discriminating against Blacks, they are **missing out on tons of Negros business**, and we have too much buying power to be left off the table. By helping us, they will be **helping themselves!**

So if you are interested in the movement, and you want to stand up, be an activist and fight for our equality, instead of sitting around speaking nonsense, then call **1-800 MNILDEW** and let's **BE ABOUT IT!**

Shawn: Well... that's about all the time we have for today's show. We will see you next week on the Shawn Show when we talk about **"The War on Drugs" when will it be over?** I'm Shawn (O'Really?) Saying Peace Out... and Keep the Faith.

---

9 months later

Broadcasting from Wolfe News

Sarah: Good Evening and welcome to the Wolfe Network (the source you can trust for unbiased reporting)... Today on the 5 o'clock news, A new anti-terrorist unit has been launched, A Black man is wanted for Armed Robbery and a little white girl is still missing... But FIRST... Some good news taking place at the **RockFeather Building** this evening. What is it Bill?

Bill: Well... I'm here at the **CNA headquarters** and there is a massive celebration going on down here. Lilly White

Model Magazine recently released it's latest issue and low and behold, **Laquita Johnson**, an African American female graces the cover. So as you can see, there is a lot of singing, dancing, and Holy Ghost music going on here. It's crazy. The police are monitoring the situation, and so far, no one has gotten hurt.

I'm here with Thomas Ad'Visor, president and CEO of **MNILDEW**, and he would like to say a few words.

Thomas: Today is a beautiful day in the Black community. It is a day of triumph, and a day of **PROGRESS**. We had a tough fight, and many **OF OUR OWN PEOPLE** were against us, but we have persevered again.

Bill: And Thomas, what you said on the Shawn (O'Really?) show certainly rings true. This issue of Lilly White has only been out for a week, and it is the **single highest grossing issue of any magazine in history**. People of **ALL RACES** are lining up in droves to buy it.

Thomas: That's absolutely right. Now, we want everyone in the local area to come out and support Lilly White. We talked about them when they were wrong, now let's support them when they are right. And... if you **buy a copy of Lilly White Magazine at full price**, you will also receive a free copy of Laquita Johnson's book, "**How I Overcame.**" I have Laquita right here with me! Laquita, tell them about your book!

Laquita: Yes, it is so powerful brothas and sistas. This book basically takes you through the process of me becoming a front cover model on Lilly White. I went through so much yall. I was getting angry and jealous stares from the other models. They taunted me, **talkin about how I have to put chemicals in my hair to make it look like theirs**. I was followed and I even received **death threats**. And that is just the beginning!

But it was worth it yall. I mean, I've done a lot of modeling in my day. I've been a jet beauty, I've been in Black Men's and Nubian Model Mag. But... (tearing up)... **there's no accomplishment like being the first Black Model in Lilly White**. I just thank God that He gave me this opportunity. And I couldn't let my people down!

Thomas: That's right, and you are so beautiful Sister.

Laquita: Thank you Tom. I couldn't have done it without you.

Bill: Well, there you have it. A beautiful day of PROGRESS in the Black Community. Back to you Sarah.

---

1 and a half years later at the Melting Pot Magazine celebration

---

Cecil: Well Mr. Charlie, what do you think of mister RockFeather now?

Charlie: I want to have his children.

Cecil: HA HA HAAA! I hope you aren't serious. (smiling)

Charlie: Mr. Mann.. just look at these numbers. Are revenue has gone up **$500,000** in less than two years! And suggesting changing the name to Melting Pot Magazine was a brilliant idea. Now, 35% of our business is coming from the Ni.. I mean... the Neg... Afro... what are we supposed to be calling these people now?

Cecil: Don't worry about it Charlie. I know who you are talking about.

Charlie: But... what's up with all of these **KKK** people outside protesting with the "**Death of Lilly White**" signs? They are freaking me out!

Cecil: Don't worry Charlie. They won't hurt you. **they are just there for a distraction**. You know... a cover. We wouldn't want people thinking this all was just some so called, "White Supremacist" plan. Get it?

Charlie: Well... No... not really, but good thinking!!

(phone rings)

Charlie: I'll get it. OH... Mr. Alex RockFeather. How Ya Doin Buddy?! I was just telling Mr. Mann how much I love you! I'm rich beyond my wildest dreams and things are only going to get better. **Alex, you really ARE Great**! Thanks and we will talk. (hangs up).

Cecil: Well Charlie, this party is wonderful. But I better leave before I get drunk and high and try to drive home. By the way, here is that Nubian Model Mag you let me borrow. I had fun with it.

Charlie: (chuckling) Thanks Cecil. Go ahead and hit the Road. But before you leave, check out this article about us in the local paper.

From the local paper.

A historical magazine that was struggling to survive 2 years ago is now flourishing. Melting Pot Magazine is now the second leading magazine in the world behind **MultiCultural Today** and is quickly moving to overtake it. Moving from a more "classical" style to a more urban approach is what Mister Charlie claims is the reason for the recent turnaround. Using a plethora of revealing and risqué photo shoots, showing women from many different cultures in different settings, the **sizzling hot** Melting Pot has encapsulated the minds of the masses!

And while he admits that he resisted it at first, Mister Charlie now realizes that **"Change" is really for the better.**

And in related news, it's a sad day for the **Marcus G**. corporation. Yesterday Mr. G announced that **Nubian Model Mag would be releasing it's last issue**. With an approximate loss of **$400,000** in revenue in the past year and a half. Marcus can no longer afford to pay the models or the employees.

When asked, what the reason was for the magazines demise, a very distraught Mr. G. gave a very strange one word response.

Progress

Victims of Progress

Negro League Baseball, Black Businesses, Black Entrepreneurship, Natural Hair, Human Rights, Black Love, Black Culture Pride, Black Consciousness, Black Liberation, Black Freedom...

"Or maybe what they say is true. Breathing in Mildew causes mental illness"

Black Radical

Peace IN!

The Brown H0rnet

Bio:

Matt Mason is the founder of Free Your Mind Online, a website designed to empower individuals so that they can take control of their personal finances and achieve wealth. This website includes a free financial e-zine, a resource center, a blog, a movie center and an e-book store.

Free Your Mind Online... And the rest will follow.
http://freeyourmindonline.net

The Brown H0rnet at Destee.com
http://www.destee.com/index.php?members/
brown_h0rnet.19140/

Racism, the Final Frontier

By **Clyde C. Coger, Jr**

At issue and spanning the globe today, which consumes the news media and daily conversations between individuals, stems the age old problem of races, racism and racialist attitudes. The larger problematic debate involves the first real Black U. S. President, Barack Obama, and not Bill Clinton; since Clinton was given to us as the first black president by our own black female author, Toni Morrison.

Rotten.com puts it this way, *"in a 1998 essay in the New Yorker, author Toni Morrison described Clinton as our first*

black president, Blacker than any actual person who could
ever be elected in our children's lifetime. She went on to say:

Clinton displays almost every trope of blackness: single-parent
household, born poor, working-class, saxophone-playing,
McDonald's-and-junk-food-loving boy from Arkansas.

This is just another reason that the Republicans absolutely
hated Clinton. He's getting votes from the minorities just for
being poor white trash fercrissakes!"

Since we now have our first real legitimate black president
in Mr. Barack Obama, racism continues to raise its ugly
head and disguises itself well inside the political efforts
of the Tea Party. No one can deny the impact of having
a real black president in this County and in this World,
has had and is absolutely devastating across the board.

Even blacks don't agree 100% with Obama's presidency;
and white people are out to hurt, harm and even kill him.
It takes elder black activist Dick Gregory to set straight
the black problem with Obama in his famous address at
Tavis Smiley's State of the Black Union Conference 2008,
in New Orleans.

Gregory made this statement:

> *"…apologize to Clinton for us tricking him by*
> *going into the big ole black pot and saying here*
> *white boy, you black, and we went back in that*

black pot telling Obama here, because you aint
black enough, what kind of fool are you (us)."

The salient point Gregory makes is clear, Clinton is a white man made black (by Morrison) and Obama is a black man, not needing pigmentation, but is considered by many blacks, not black enough; Gregory then goes on to correctly state, *"The KKK hasn't done to Obama what we have."*

Is perceived racism on solid ground?

Well…With recent governmental scientific discovery on human lineage, the Genome Project, through the use of **Mt DNA** (**mitochondrial**); it has been determined that all 7 billion people of the earth's population trace back to indigenous African people in Africa, by blood.

This important fact finally makes clear that black people can no longer be considered inferior, and that white people are definitely not superior, in fact, they are mutant recessives spun from originally created black people. Biologically, Racism is now a non-issue.

Therefore my people, read and enjoy the poem by sister phynxofkmt, *Mystery of History*, which is located at the end of this book; because, our mental liberation is now here…Jubilee to the people, come out of the belly of the beast.

Clyde C. Coger, Jr.

Bio:
Author of the Book: Does Color Matter? Only When Misrepresented: The Bible depicts the Colors of Man and Consequences of false Representation
www.clydecoger.com

Rotten.com http://www.rotten.com/library/bio/presidents/bill-clinton/

Dick Gregory apologizes to the first Black President http://www.youtube.com/watch?v=JAcN5iKArQU

Humble Beginnings of the GroupThink Project-Group (GT) http://destee.com/forums/showthread.php?t=56440&page=2

CHAPTER 6

DESTEE NETWORK

One of the most important steps in the quest for wealth consciousness in the Black community is to understand that we already generate plenty of wealth! In America, we spend close to a trillion dollars per year. Unfortunately, over 95% of that money goes outside of our community. This is the reason for the Destee Network. We need to start to support our own. And we need a central place where we can come together and do so.

Visit the **Destee Network** and shop Black.

http://www.destee.com/network/

SUGGESTED READING AND/OR VIEWING

Historical Perspective

- **Stolen Legacy**: George G.M. Games
- **Nile Valley Contributions to Civilization (Exploding the Myths)** by Anthony T. Browder
- **Destruction of Black Civilization: Great Issues of a Race from 4500 B.C to 2000 A.D.** by Chancellor Williams
- **Does Color Matter? Only When Misrepresented!: the Bible depicts the Colors of Man and Consequences of false Representation** by Clyde C. Coger Jr.
- **Blacked Out Through Whitewash: Exposing the Quantum Deception/Rediscovering and Recovering Suppressed Melanated** by Suzar and Suzar
- **Ancient Future** by Wayne B. Chandler
- **Skull and Bones - Illuminati Resurrected** http://daghettotymz.com/rkyvz/articles/skull&bones/s&b1.html

- **America's Secret Establishment**: An Introduction to the Order of Skull & Bones by Antony C. Sutton

Health Related

- **Sugar Blues** by William F. Duffy
- **The Chemical Feminization and Castration of Men** by Curtis Duncan: http://www.drcurtisduncan.com/2012/03/chemical-feminization-and-emasculation.html
- **Harmed By Hormones: How Estrogenic Chemicals Make Women Fat, Sick, and Infertile** by Curtis Duncan: http://www.drcurtisduncan.com/2012/03/chemical-feminization-and-emasculation.html
- **The Anti-Estrogenic Diet**: How Estrogenic Foods and Chemicals Are Making You Fat and Sick by Ori Hofmekler
- **The Disappearing Male**: http://informationliberation.com/?id=26130
- **Murder by Injection: The Story of the Medical Conspiracy Against America** by Eustace Mullins
- **The Pimp Juice Conspiracy** by Matt Mason: http://freeyourmindonline.net/Blog/2008/03/the-pimp-juice-conspiracy/

Wealth Consciousness

- **The Master Key System** by Charles Haanel
- **The Science of Getting Rich** by Wallace Wattles

- **The Law of Success in 16 Lessons** by Napoleon Hill
- **The Money, Wealth and Prosperity Manual Vol. 1** by Djehuty Ma'at-Ra: http://www.dhealthstore.com/the-money-wealth-prosperity-manual-vol-1.html
- **Think And Grow Rich** by Napoleon Hill
- **Rich Dad's Advisors: Guide to Investing In Gold and Silver**: Protect Your Financial Future by Michael Maloney
- **Ebony Experiment:** http://www.youtube.com/watch?v=8XhZD1o_vNg
- **Why Blacks are doomed to struggle financially? (Djehuty Maat Ra)** http://destee.com/forums/showthread.php?t=61238

Other Notables

- **What Black Men Think** by Producer Janks Morton http://whatblackmenthink.com/
- **Conspiracy Documentaries:** http://freeyourmindonline.net/Infotainment.html
- **Caucasian Albinos** http://destee.com/index.php?threads/caucasian-albinos.44504/
- **Should Black People Unite Regardless of Religion?** http://destee.com/forums/showthread.php?t=61976

CONCLUSION

Front Cover Image of Malcolm X

Drawn by: Clyde C. Coger, Jr
2-15-2013
Malcolm X in February 1965
(Michael Dehs archives)

My humble beginnings of first hearing the full talks of Brother Malcolm on LP's, together with our "*homegrown*" publication material, inspired me to produce a "*homegrown*" image for use rather than familiar snapshots. The personal touch points to Malcolm's originality as well. And the popular phrase, ***by any means necessary***, mirror's the serious look on his face captured in the drawing of a photo taken sometime in February,

1965; the month and year of his assassination. Hence, 48 years later, we pay tribute to our finest, fearless leader, El Hajj Malik El-Shabazz.

Clyde C. Coger, Jr.

BIBLIOGRAPHY

Introduction

- **African Management Methods – benefits** (http://www.referenceforbusiness.com/ encyclopedia/A-Ar/African-Management-Methods.html#ixzz1995v5fxb)
- **Speech: Message to the Grass Roots**, Malcolm X, Encyclopedia Britannica
- **W.E.B. Dubois Learning Center** http://www. duboislc.net/SankofaMeaning.html

Chapter 1

- **The Concise Oxford English Dictionary**
- **The Oxford Companion of The English Language**
- **Dr. Claude Anderson, PowerNomics**: The National Plan to Empower Black America
- Dr. Amos Wilson: **How White Society Promotes Violence in the Afrikan** Community http:// www.youtube.com/watch?v=WZSIe5oTqSs

- **The Isis Papers**: The Keys to the Colors by Frances Cress Welsing
- Ochberg, Frank "**The Ties That Bind Captive to Captor**": The "Stockholm Syndrome"

Chapter 2

- **America's Secret Establishment**: An Introduction to the Order of Skull & Bones by Antony C. Sutton
- **Skull and Bones - Illuminati Resurrected** http://daghettotymz.com/rkyvz/articles/skull&bones/s&b1.html
- Springmeier, Fritz: **Bloodlines of the Illuminati**
- **Election Update, Should You Vote?** http://freeyourmindonline.net/Blog/2008/08/election-update-should-you-vote/
- **Presidential Bloodlines** http://ericdubay.hubpages.com/hub/bloodlines
- Wes Penre: **The Secret Order of the Illuminati** http://www.illuminati-news.com/moriah.htm#2
- **Do The Illuminati Run The Street Gangs?** http://www.youtube.com/watch?v=rNBjDFH7QLc
- **Masonry - The Root of Global White Supremacy** http://daghettotymz.com/rkyvz/articles/masonry/masonry1/masonrypt1.html
- **The History of the House of Rothschild** http://www.iamthewitness.com/DarylBradfordSmith_Rothschild.htm

- **Skull & Bones Photo taken by Erin Callaway** (http://www.freeimages.com/profile/kalierin)

Chapter 4

- **Ebony Experiment** (You Tube video of John and Maggie Anderson) http://www.youtube.com/watch?v=8XhZD1o_vNg
- Amos Wilson breaking down Racism and making it clear and plain http://www.youtube.com/user/Afrikanl...88/j38A58yLcOQ
- Marcia Wade Talbert, BLACK ENTERPRISE: **Anderson s Complete Year of 'Buying Black'** (The Empowerment Experiment --formerly the Ebony Experiment --) http://www.blackenterprise.com/files/2010/01/09WFL-Anderson-LIVE2EXC.jpg
- Fluoride, **WATER FILTRATION AND PURIFICATION PRODUCTS**: Fluoridated Water - Dental Fluorosis http://www.tuberose.com/Fluoride.html
- **The Fluoride Glut**: Sources of Fluoride Exposure http://www.fluoridealert.org/f-sources.htm
- **Notes on Fluorine/Fluoride Detoxification**
- Paul Fassa, citizen journalist: **How to Detox Fluorides from Your Body** http://www.naturalnews.com/026605_fl...des_detox.html
- Maria Abdin: **Notes on Fluorine/Fluoride Detoxification** http://www.tldp.com/issue/202/Notes_Fluorine.htm

- **The Chemical Feminization and Castration of Men** by Curtis Duncan http://www.drcurtisduncan.com/2012/03/chemical-feminization-and-emasculation.html
- **The Anti-Estrogenic Diet**: How Estrogenic Foods and Chemicals Are Making You Fat and Sick by Ori Hofmekler
- **The Disappearing Male**: http://informationliberation.com/?id=26130

Chapter 5

- http://www.rotten.com/library/bio/presidents/bill-clinton/
- Dick Gregory apologizes to the first Black President http://www.youtube.com/watch?v=JAcN5iKArQU

Chapter 6

- **DESTEE** *Discussion Forum* http://destee.com/
- **Black People Web Sites**...(Destee Network) http://destee.com/network
- Poem: *Mystery in History*, copyright...by sister phynxofkmt http://destee.com/forums/showpost.php?p=586267

Mystery in history

Long ago, some people lived in caves
Stayed so long their skin began to fade
Along with it went, the melanin tint
That would indicate the source
from where they came
Their hair went straight
Missed the melanin kink
And the pineal gland calcified
how they did think

In the pit of the cavern
in the deep of the night
the story began
for those they call white

White people, cave people
put down your guns
We understand why you hide
from the sun
For home you yearn, but
exposed you burn
and it's no secret you
used to be one of US

White people, white people
stop all this war
possession, consumption
won't heal the core

White people, cave people
put down the guns
then, only then can u
return to the one

White people, cave people,
put down the weapons
and stop the pretense that
we're the burden
The affliction is yours
of degenerative health
but you cover it up
by using your wealth
wealth that you steal
wealth that you owe
wealth that you eat
and make others sow

White people, white people
stop being afraid
start building on truth
and pull down the facade
of ethics in politics
honest econo-trix
plunder to commercialize
bottle and label cultural pride

So that you too can feel
what it means to be real
really proud and really you

and really true
to the meaning of love within
peace for all and....

Yes, white people can yoga
chant, meditate and pray
in earnest and prostrate
before GOD
but you still came from
and are derived from
the same spark of
the life's sun
AS US

http://destee.com/forums/showpost.php?p=586267
copyright...by sister phynxofkmt